Great Short Stories
Synopses, Quizzes, and Tests

Aileen M. Carroll

J. Weston Walch, Publisher
Portland, Maine

1   2   3   4   5   6   7   8   9   10

ISBN 0-8251-1497-7

Copyright © 1989
J. Weston Walch, Publisher
P.O. Box 658 • Portland, Maine 04104-0658

Printed in the United States of America

Contents

Unit 4. Survival: Stories of Adventure and Danger in the Outdoors 73

Unit 5. The Many Faces of Love 97

Unit 6. Tales with a Twist: Get Ready for Some Surprise Endings 121

Unit 7.   The Way We Were: Stories That Are Glimpses of the Past 145

Unit 8.   The Values We Cherish: Stories of Faith, Courage, Loyalty, and Generosity 169

Unit 9.   Chillers and Thrillers: Stories of Mystery, Murder, and the Supernatural 191

Unit 13.   Exploring the Hidden World of the Mind: Stories to Help You

Understand Why People Behave As They Do 283

Unit 14.   Another Point of View: Stories to Help You Look

at the World in a New Way 305

Unit 15.   They Dared to Stand Up and Be Counted: Stories of People with

Courage and Conviction 327

To the Teacher

150 Great Short Stories is designed to be used as a teaching aid, either in the classroom as an adjunct to standard anthologies, or in an "outside reading" program to help you and your students select suitable stories for their reading level and interests.

Using *150 Great Short Stories* in the classroom

Because *150 Great Short Stories* includes many of the commonly anthologized stories, it is ideal for classroom use. For each story, the following format is used: for the teacher, a brief *synopsis* so that the story can be reviewed quickly; a *suggestion* for teaching that particular story; an *answer key* for the reading quiz; and for the students, a *reading quiz* which, generally, has the same emphasis as the *suggestion* and is appropriate to the story's content and level of difficulty.

The teacher suggestions may cover one or more of the many facets of the short story, such as characterization, setting, plot, and theme. Some suggestions address the analysis of such writing techniques as first-person point of view, sense appeal, dialect, metaphor, simile, and symbolism. These suggestions can be used as the basis for class discussions or for writing assignments.

The reading quizzes vary in format; they include sentence completion, short essay, matching, and identification of quotations from the story. Some are open-book, encouraging students to read for significance. Others are library oriented, so that students can practice finding information in standard reference books. A few quizzes stress vocabulary, if the story has a foreign flavor or contains words students may not have met before.

Using *150 Great Short Stories* as a sourcebook

If *150 Great Short Stories* will be used primarily as a sourcebook for outside reading assignments, the suggestions will be useful for discussing a story with a student or putting together a written assignment based on a story. If you prefer a "reading check," the quiz will work well, allowing students to judge whether or not they have grasped the significant points of the story.

A few words on the format

Stories are classified into thematic categories designed to appeal to young readers and help you and the students decide which stories are best suited to them. A detailed Table of Contents appears at the beginning of each category. It lists a source for each short story, indicates the stories which deal with a particular nationality or ethnic group, and states the level of difficulty of every story. The categories are listed in order of difficulty, from the easiest to the most demanding.

Each story in each category is designated as *easy*, *moderate*, or *difficult*. A few stories are classified as *easy to moderate* or *moderate to difficult*. For this labeling, several factors were taken into consideration:

A story is labeled *difficult* if its concept is a demanding one for teenagers, given their limited reading and life experience; if the author's style and vocabulary are especially challenging; and if the story has subtlety, irony, or ambiguity which young readers might find confusing. You will find that for such stories, the suggestion is designed to help you to present them in a way that will make them easier for students to understand. (Fewer than ten stories out of the entire collection are labeled *difficult*.)

The same criteria were used for labeling a story as *moderate* in difficulty, but these stories are less demanding and should present few problems to average or above-average students. Again, your use of the suggestions in the classroom or with an individual student on an independent reading assignment will make the story more memorable. (About one third of the stories fall into the *moderate* classification.)

The remaining stories, nearly one hundred, are classified as *easy*, and the reading quizzes are designed accordingly. In most of the fifteen thematic categories, "easy" stories predominate. Some were chosen for slower readers, but all were selected to give students a pleasurable and worthwhile reading experience so they will have a good introduction to the wonderfully varied world of the short story.

The quizzes

An important consideration in designing quizzes for this book was that they be easy to grade. Therefore, students are instructed to answer sentence-completion questions in the fewest possible words, and to write only one carefully worded sentence if a short-essay answer is required. Answers to matching exercises involving only a letter are kept to the left-hand margin, as are the one- or two-word answers.

The bibliography and indexes

So that you or the school librarians need not waste valuable research time locating a particular short story, a bibliography is included, listing one source for every story. Of course, the most commonly anthologized stories may already appear in classroom texts. If a story does not appear in a classroom text, and if your school library does not have one of the source books listed in the bibliography, you might have to consult the *Short Story Index* to locate a story which particularly interests you or your students.

You may decide to have the students do the library sleuthing and make their own selections. If so, just photocopy the bibliography so that each student can browse in the library whenever time allows. As an alternative, the librarian might be willing to set up a short-story anthology display from which students can select story collections or individual stories that interest them.

Finally, as another aid to selection, an index of authors is included so that a student interested in a particular writer can check easily to see which of his or her stories is included in *150 Great Short Stories*. Similarly, an index of stories is included so that students can easily look up a title.

UNIT 1

GROWING PAINS ════════════════════

Making the Transition from Childhood to Adulthood

UNIT 1

GROWING PAINS

Making the Transition from Childhood to Adulthood 1

Bad Characters

Jean Stafford

Easy

<u>SYNOPSIS</u>

The narrator, Emily Vanderpool, lives with her parents, brother, and sisters. She is a lonely eleven-year-old, not on good terms with her siblings and apt to alienate others with her "terrible" talent for "invective." Alone at home one day, she finds a strange girl, Lottie Jump, stealing a chocolate cake from the kitchen. Lottie, a new girl in town, impresses Emily, and she is pleased when Lottie asks her to be "pals," but she must help Lottie to shoplift. On their first excursion, Lottie does the actual stealing, but when she is caught, she blames Emily and plays deaf and dumb to gain sympathy. In the end, Emily has learned her lesson and curbs her tongue to keep worthwhile friends.

<u>SUGGESTION</u>

In a class discussion, students should decide what Emily's problem is. (She wants affection and approval, but is thoughtless and inconsiderate.) Ask them if she is really a "bad" character.

ANSWER KEY

1. Polecat
2. Muff the cat
3. punishment
4. guilt
5. Adams, Colorado
6. tall, pinched, and pasty
7. Oklahoma
8. Comanche Café
9. part Indian
10. TB
11. stealing
12. perfume flask
13. rubber gloves
14. raw potatoes
15. making a snowman
16. "Kid"
17. candy
18. chocolate cake
19. hat
20. rude

3

Name: _____

Date: _____

Bad Characters

In this exercise, you must select the correct word or words from the list below to complete each of the twenty statements.

Muff the cat	Adams, Colorado	Comanche Café
raw potatoes	perfume flask	tall, pinched, and pasty
hat	rubber gloves	candy
chocolate cake	making a snowman	guilty
Oklahoma	"Kid"	TB
punishment	part Indian	Polecat
stealing	rude	

1. _____ Emily's brother's name for her was _____ .

2. _____ Although Emily insulted people and lost their friendship, through it all she could count on _____ .

3. _____ Her father's friend, Judge Bay, frightened her with his talk of _____ for wrongdoers.

4. _____ Emily knew she was somewhat to blame because things were going badly at her house. It was _____ that caused her tantrum.

5. _____ The story takes place in _____ .

6. _____ In appearance, Lottie Jump was _____ .

7. _____ Lottie came from _____ .

8. _____ Lottie's mother worked in the _____ .

9. _____ Lottie said her mother was _____ .

(continued)

Bad Characters (continued)

10. _____   Lottie's father had _____ .

11. _____   Lottie's skill and recreation was _____ .

12. _____   After Lottie's visit, Emily's mother couldn't find her _____ .

13. _____   When Lottie asked Emily what she'd like, Emily blurted out, "_____ ."

14. _____   Emily was a fussy eater with a fondness for _____ .

15. _____   While they were _____ , Emily insulted Virgil Meade.

16. _____   Lottie's name for Emily was _____ .

17. _____   After she was caught stealing, the men felt sorry for Lottie because they thought she was deaf and dumb. They gave her _____ .

18. _____   When Emily and Lottie met, Lottie was about to steal a _____ .

19. _____   Lottie hid all the things she had stolen in her _____ .

20. _____   Emily's fault was being _____ to others.

Almos' a Man

Richard Wright

Easy

SYNOPSIS

Dave, a seventeen-year-old black, works in the fields like a man, but is still treated like a boy. His dream is to own a gun, the symbol for him of manhood. The storekeeper will sell him an old pistol for $2.00, but first he must persuade his mother to give him that much, for she handles his pay. On the first day he has the gun, he accidentally shoots his employer's mule. When he finally admits what he has done, the owner says he must pay $50.00 for the dead mule, and everyone laughs at him. Frustrated, he retrieves the gun from its hiding place, shoots it, and hops a freight train to go where he will be treated like a man.

SUGGESTION

Some students may find that the dialect in "Almos' a Man" interferes with their understanding of the story. A discussion of the advantages and disadvantages of a writer's using dialect would be worthwhile—it adds authenticity but may interfere with clarity. Also, the author must have an "ear" for dialect to reproduce the sounds correctly, and he always runs the risk of seeming to patronize the people whose dialect he is using.

ANSWER KEY

1. Dave	6. Jim Hawkins	11. Ma
2. Jenny	7. Dave	12. Ma
3. Mistah Joe	8. Pa	13. Dave
4. Ma	9. Dave	14. Pa
5. Jim Hawkins	10. Mistah Joe	15. Dave

Name: _____

Date: _____

Almos' a Man

Match the characters in Column A with the descriptions in Column B. Some names are used more than once.

Column A

Dave

Ma

Pa

Mistah Joe

Jenny

Jim Hawkins

Column B

1. _____ At seventeen, almos' a man

2. _____ The victim of poor marksmanship

3. _____ Owner of the village store

4. _____ Handles the seventeen-year-old's pay

5. _____ Is the seventeen-year-old's employer

6. _____ Owns the dead mule

7. _____ Finally hops a freight train

8. _____ Threatens to beat the seventeen-year-old

Now match the speech below with a speaker from Column A.

9. _____ "Ah jus wanted t see ef yuhd lemme look at tha ol catalog erwhile."

10. _____ "Oh, it's kinda old . . . A pistol. A big one."

11. _____ "You git up from there and git to the well n wash yosef! Ah ain feeden no hogs in mah house!"

12. _____ "N ef yo pa jus though Ah let yuh have money t buy a gun he'd hava fit."

13. _____ "Lissen here, Jenny! When ah pull this ol trigger Ah don wan yah t run n acka fool now."

14. _____ "Yuh wan me t take a tree lim n beat yuh till yuh talk!"

15. _____ "Lawd, ef Ah had jus one mo bullet, Ah'd taka shot at tha house . . . Jussa enough t let im know Ah'm a man."

150 Great Short Stories

Kintu

Elizabeth Enright

Easy

SYNOPSIS

Kintu, son of an African chief, lives in the jungle with his family. As the eldest son, Kintu has many lessons to learn, for someday he too will be a chief. Secretly, Kintu is afraid of the jungle, but knows he will be expected to hunt and show no fear. Troubled, he visits the witch doctor, whose cure for Kintu's fear is to send him alone into the jungle to plant a charm beneath a baobab tree. Following those instructions, Kintu gets lost, and the snarl of a leopard sends him scrambling up a tree. When the leopard follows, Kintu throws his spear as his father taught him. He kills the leopard and his fear.

SUGGESTION

The students need to recognize that "Kintu" is the story of a boy's passage into manhood. Facing his fear and his danger, he reacts with skill and courage and emerges triumphant.

ANSWER KEY

1. D, F	6. H
2. E	7. B, G
3. C	8. A
4. D, F	9. J
5. G, D	10. I

Reading Quiz:
A Boy Grows Up

Name: _____

Date: _____

Kintu

In this quiz, Column A contains Kintu's various actions and reactions. Your task is to select from Column B the quality which each of these actions or reactions reveals. (Some may require more than one choice.)

Column A

1. _____ Kintu's daily practice of spear-throwing and arrow-shooting

2. _____ Kintu's admission to himself that it would never do for a chief's son to be afraid

3. _____ Kintu's visiting the witch doctor

4. _____ Kintu's carrying out the witch doctor's instructions

5. _____ Kintu's going deeper into the jungle to find a baobab tree

6. _____ Kintu's following the monkeys and climbing the tree

7. _____ Kintu's hurling the spear and killing the leopard

8. _____ Kintu's momentary sadness over the death of the leopard

9. _____ Kintu's decision that it is better to kill than to be killed

10. _____ Kintu's mood as he returns to the village

Column B

A. compassion

B. self-control

C. trust and faith

D. persistence

E. sense of responsibility

F. determination to succeed

G. courage

H. resourcefulness

I. self-confidence

J. good sense

150 Great Short Stories

The Doll's House

Katherine Mansfield   *Easy*

SYNOPSIS

The Burnell daughters have the greatest influence in the little village school. In fact, Isabel, the oldest of the three, holds court at recess. The Kelveys, Lil and Else, are at the other end of the social scale and, as outsiders, are ignored or taunted. When an elderly friend gives the Burnells a doll house, completely furnished, they invite school chums home, two each day, to see it. Of course, the Kelveys are not included. But one day, Kezia Burnell sees the Kelveys passing and, on impulse, invites them in. When her aunt discovers the intruders, they are driven out, but they are contented to have seen the doll's house.

SUGGESTION

In this brief short story, Katherine Mansfield shows the snobbery and cruelty of young girls who, actually, are reflecting their elders' attitudes. Ask the students to cite incidents from the story that reveal adult prejudice. (For example, the teacher's attitude toward the Kelveys.)

ANSWER KEY

1. B	6. G
2. A	7. I
3. D	8. H
4. E	9. C
5. F	10. H

Name: _____

Date: _____

The Doll's House

If you can match the description in Column A with the name in Column B, you know what kind of person each character in the story is.

Column A

1. _____ Was inclined to be bossy because she was the eldest

2. _____ Was kinder than her sisters

3. _____ Was a sweet and generous old lady

4. _____ Considered themselves better than everyone else

5. _____ Had no social standing and were very humble

6. _____ Taunted the outcasts of the playground

7. _____ Was shy and clung to her sister, but wanted to see the doll's house, as any little girl would

8. _____ Was a realist who knew that her family was not socially acceptable

9. _____ Was harsh and scolding to the poor little girls who had been invited into the courtyard

10. _____ Politely gave flowers to her teacher, who did not appreciate them

Column B

A. Kezia

B. Isabel

C. Aunt Beryl

D. Mrs. Hay

E. the Burnell family

F. the Kelvey family

G. Lena Logan

H. Lil

I. Else

Paul's Case

Willa Cather   *Moderate*

SYNOPSIS

Paul is a "difficult" boy, continually at odds with his teachers for insolence and indifference, often annoying his father with his late hours and lack of ambition. Only as a concert-hall usher or hanger-on at the theater does Paul feel happy, transported from the everyday world he despises. Finally, Paul's father takes him out of school and puts him to work. By doing so, he unwittingly gives Paul an entrée to the world he dreams about. Paul steals $2000 of company funds and has a glorious few days in New York before he is tracked down. Then he takes what he thinks is the only possible way out for him—suicide.

SUGGESTION

Students generally find Paul fascinating. He is a nonconformist, determined to reject the reality of his workaday world and live his romantic fantasy. A good classroom discussion can be based on whether Paul was a victim of his environment or of his own inability to face reality.

ANSWER KEY

1. strangely glittering eyes; narrow shoulders
2. Asleep, Paul looked like a troubled old man; there was something haunted about him.
3. He "loses" himself, is enraptured.
4. same as the paintings
5. irritable and let down, forced to return to dull reality
6. It is respectable and dull.
7. accounts of wealthy men and their way of life, the world he'd like to enter
8. Answers will vary. (Make-believe world has everything his real world lacks.)
9. living out his fantasy
10. had a revolver, but couldn't use it

Name: _____

Date: _____

Paul's Case

For this exercise, you'll need to reread certain paragraphs to find the answers to the questions and the clues you need to understand Paul. Make your answers *brief*.

1. What about Paul's appearance sets him apart? What physical characteristic is he embarrassed about?

   _____

   _____

2. What did the drawing teacher remember about Paul that made him feel that Paul's teachers didn't understand him?

   _____

   _____

3. What effect does the picture gallery at the concert hall have on Paul?

   _____

   _____

4. What effect does the symphony have?

   _____

   _____

5. How does he feel after the concert, and why does he feel that way?

   _____

   _____

(continued)

Paul's Case (continued)

6. Why does Paul's neighborhood repel him?

   _____

   _____

7. What part of the Sunday-afternoon stories does Paul enjoy?

   _____

   _____

8. In Cather's words, "the stage entrance of that theater was for Paul the actual portal of Romance." What do you think she means?

   _____

   _____

9. How does Paul spend the stolen money?

   _____

   _____

10. His suicide was premeditated. How did he actually prepare for waking up from his dream?

    _____

    _____

The Runaway

Morley Callaghan
Easy

SYNOPSIS

Michael is an adolescent, big for his age, confused, and unhappy. He is the first to jump off a roof into a sawdust pile, daring the other boys to follow, but the second time around, he can't bring himself to jump, and they call him "yellow." At home, his stepmother reprimands him, but his big, kindly father tries to restore his confidence. Then the parents quarrel over him, and Michael hopes no passersby hear the argument. Trying to prove himself, he beats up a black boy, new in the neighborhood, then makes friends with him. Back home, he finds his mother praying and his father sitting in the woodshed, dejected. Refused by a girl he likes, he runs away, looking for a new life.

SUGGESTION

Callaghan's realistic portrayal of Michael leaves the readers with some questions because there is no "pat" solution, no happy ending to this short story. A good classroom discussion should emerge from an attempt to analyze why Michael is running away. Certainly, he sees himself as the cause of friction between his parents, but what are some other reasons for his actions?

ANSWER KEY

1. feels partly to blame that parents quarrel, dislikes friction

2. Apparently, Joe's life is free and adventurous.

3. Answers will vary.

4. He's not sure of really being accepted and fears they may have heard his parents arguing.

5. to save face with his friends

6. People are talking about him and his family.

7. afraid his father may have done something desperate

8. starting over, an exciting life in the city

The Runaway

Answer each question with one carefully worded sentence.

1. In his own mind, how does Michael justify running away?

   _____

   _____

2. What in his Uncle Joe's way of life fascinates Michael?

   _____

   _____

3. Why do you think Michael had to force himself to jump the second time?

   _____

   _____

4. Why doesn't Michael walk home with Helen and her mother when Helen invites him?

   _____

   _____

5. Why does Michael fight the black boy?

   _____

   _____

6. What does Michael fear is taking place in all the neighbors' houses?

   _____

   _____

7. Why is he afraid to go into the woodshed?

   _____

   _____

8. What is he anticipating as he leaves town?

   _____

   _____

Prongs

L.A.G. Strong

Easy

SYNOPSIS

Twelve-year-old Dan is watching eight-year-old Johnny, who is so interested in fishing prawns from a rock pool that he won't go home. Dan knows that if they are late for supper, he'll be the one to get the "belt" from their father. When Dan tries to drag Johnny away, they fight. A loafer intervenes and knocks Dan down. But when the boys say Jem Foster is their father, to make amends, he offers them a little money, which they take in exchange for the "prongs." To turn aside Jem's anger, the boys say they were catching prawns to sell. Jem takes the money for a drink, and peace is restored for the moment.

SUGGESTION

A good exercise for students who read this story is to have them say what is the first adjective that comes to mind to describe "Prongs." Some answers might be *humorous, unusual, true-to-life,* but *violent* is perhaps the most appropriate, considering the loafer's violence to Dan, the father's to his children, and even the boys' to each other.

ANSWER KEY

1. ragged coat . . . many sizes too big

2. sulkily handsome

3. hated

4. local nondescripts

5. ecstasy of rage

6. affectionate, warm-hearted

7. a bad man to cross, a bad man to quarrel with

8. father scowls, mother's face shows pale

9. piteous relief

10. Dan, thoughtful; Johnny, contented to be with his brother

Prongs

1. _____   In the second and third paragraphs of the story, what words indicate that Johnny is from a poor family? (6 words)
   _____

2. _____   What two words in the description of Dan suggest that he is not a happy boy?

3. _____   What word summarizes Dan's feeling for his father?

4. _____   What two words describe the men who saw Dan and Johnny fighting?

5. _____   What three words describe Johnny's emotion after the man kicked Dan?

6. _____   As Dan reflects while Johnny is fishing, what two words about his brother's disposition come to his mind?

7. _____   When the man finds out that Dan is Jem Foster's boy, what comes to his mind about Foster? (5 or 6 words)
   _____

8. _____   What words describe each parent's reaction when the boys arrive home very late?

9. _____   When the father takes the money and doesn't beat the boys, what two words describe the mother's reaction?

10. _____   Use your own words to describe briefly the mood of the two boys in the final paragraph of the story.

Charles

Shirley Jackson   *Easy*

<u>SYNOPSIS</u>

Laurie's mother explains that his first day at kindergarten marks the end of his "sweet-voiced" babyhood and the beginning of his swaggering boyhood. Each day, Laurie comes home from school with a tale of Charles, the bad actor of the class. Laurie's parents are so fascinated by the variety of misdemeanors Charles commits that they eagerly await the first PTA meeting and a chance to meet his mother. But no one at the meeting looks "haggard enough." When Laurie's mother talks with the teacher, however, she learns, to her surprise, that Laurie had trouble "adjusting," but is doing better, despite "occasional lapses," and no one in the class is named Charles!

<u>SUGGESTION</u>

"Charles" is brief enough so that it could be read in class and used as the basis of a discussion. Students might like to share their first-day-of-school experiences, or they might analyze why certain children try to be the center of attention by acting as the class clown or the class miscreant.

ANSWER KEY

1. B	6. D
2. B	7. C
3. F	8. E
4. H	9. G
5. A	10. I

Charles

In this exercise, if you can match Laurie's action in Column A with his reason for acting that way in Column B, you understand how he felt as he began his school days (and maybe you remember how you felt too!). Note: Some of the reasons in Column B may be used twice.

Column A

1. _____ Laurie tries the "look up, look down" routine on his father.

2. _____ Laurie comes into the house slamming doors and shouting.

3. _____ Laurie describes Charles as "bigger than me," and says Charles doesn't have to wear his rubbers and jacket.

4. _____ Laurie rejects corduroy overalls with bibs in favor of jeans with a belt.

5. _____ Laurie points out that the teacher said, "We were not to take the name of the Lord in vain."

6. _____ Laurie fills his wagon with mud and pulls it through the kitchen.

7. _____ Charles (Laurie) passed out the crayons and picked up the books after class.

8. _____ Laurie whispers the bad word to his father.

9. _____ Laurie reports that when Charles stayed after school, the other children did too.

10. _____ Charles (Laurie) misbehaved in school.

Column B

A. He was impressed by the new person in authority.

B. He was being "fresh" to show his independence.

C. He was learning to assume responsibility.

D. He was reverting to his "spoiled baby" behavior.

E. He was testing his father to see if certain language was acceptable.

F. He was showing his insecurity by making Charles the person that he wanted to be.

G. He was showing his need to be accepted by others—in this case, his classmates.

H. He was trying to appear "grown up."

I. Laurie craved attention and wanted to feel important.

Mr Tennyson

William Trevor

Easy

SYNOPSIS

Jenny, fifteen and a senior at Foxfield Comprehensive, is infatuated with her English teacher, Mr. Tennyson, and dreams about him constantly. All the senior girls know of his affair with a former student, Sarah Spence. That makes him even more glamorous to Jenny. She is certain his wife and children are burdens holding him back from his true career as a poet. Meanwhile, a classmate, Chinny Martin, the pimply owner of a Yamaha, begs her to take a ride; Chinny tells Jenny he loves her, but she rejects him. When Mr. Tennyson keeps Jenny after class to talk about her theme, she blurts out her love and hears the real and tragic story of Sarah Spence.

SUGGESTION

The closing sentence of "Mr Tennyson" contains irony, which the students should be able to recognize. Jenny, having just left Mr. Tennyson, hears Chinny Martin calling out to her, "silly with his silly love." Of course, the readers see what she does not, that her infatuation for her teacher was equally hopeless and silly.

ANSWER KEY

1. Only the senior girls know; they protect him by not telling.

2. He must be unhappily married.

3. that there have been others since Sarah

4. Sarah was the only one. She had to have an abortion and now hates him.

5. shabby

6. Other girls probably threw themselves at him too, and he discouraged them by telling the story of Sarah.

7. loved her, still does, welcomes the chance to talk about her

Name: _____

Date: _____

Mr Tennyson

Answer each of the following in one carefully worded sentence.

1. Why hasn't Mr. Tennyson's love affair with a student caused his dismissal?

   _____

   _____

2. How do the girls excuse the affair even though he is married and has children?

   _____

   _____

3. What do they suspect about him?

   _____

   _____

4. What is the truth, as he tells it?

   _____

   _____

5. What adjective does Mr. Tennyson use to describe his treatment of Sarah? (You need only one word.)

   _____

6. What unpleasant realization does Jenny have as a result of her conversation with Mr. Tennyson?

   _____

   _____

7. How did Mr. Tennyson really feel about Sarah?

   _____

   _____

Downstairs at Fitzgerald's

William Trevor   *Moderate*

SYNOPSIS

The setting is Dublin, Ireland, in the 1940's. Cecilia, whose parents divorced when she was four, is now nearly thirteen and lives with her mother and stepfather, Ronan. She spends Saturdays with her own father, who takes her to Fitzgerald's Oyster Bar, then to the movies, the races, or perhaps a museum. She loves these outings and pictures herself grown up and keeping house for her father. Then a schoolmate, Abrahamson, sows doubt in Cecilia's mind, hinting that Ronan had an affair with her mother before the divorce and that she is actually Ronan's child. Cecilia feels like crying when she leaves her father now, knowing the suspicion will always be there and fearing that he has it too.

SUGGESTION

In this short story, the author, for the most part, shows Cecilia's father through her eyes. Ask the students to supply adjectives to describe his appearance and his character—for example, *easy-going, generous,* and *inclined to make the best of things.* Ask them too if they can demonstrate from the text that he has nobility of character.

ANSWER KEY

1. B	6. A	11. D
2. B, D	7. A	12. B
3. B	8. F	13. A
4. B	9. F	14. C
5. B	10. E	15. A

Downstairs at Fitzgerald's

Match the descriptions in Column A with the characters in Column B.

Column A

1. _____ Has race-track wisdom which his friends value

2. _____ Once were business partners (two letters)

3. _____ Once owned a Morris, but has no car now

4. _____ Appears to prefer the Oyster Bar to the dining room

5. _____ Gossips a bit, but is neither malicious nor pitying

6. _____ Is the only child at the school whose parents are divorced

7. _____ For a special reason, wishes she had freckles

8. _____ Mentions that the fees are overdue and asks Cecilia to speak to her father

9. _____ Inquires about Cecilia's "family trouble"

10. _____ Is famous for his brains, but keeps to himself

11. _____ Is very thin, with a craggy face and languid mouth

12. _____ Goes from pub to pub because he is lonely

13. _____ Buys cakes from someone whether she wants to or not

14. _____ Is petite and dark-haired, like Claudette Colbert

15. _____ Now has a doubt which mars her relationship with someone she loves

Column B

A. Cecilia

B. her father

C. her mother

D. her stepfather, Ronan

E. Abrahamson, Cecilia's classmate

F. the Headmaster

UNIT 2

STORIES TO MAKE
YOU CHUCKLE

Humor and Tall Tales

UNIT 2

STORIES TO MAKE YOU CHUCKLE

The Celebrated Jumping Frog of Calaveras County

Mark Twain   *Easy*

SYNOPSIS

The narrator claims to be telling a story once told to him by Simon Wheeler about a man, Jim Smiley, who loved to bet. Smiley had a horse that won him money, and a bull pup named Andrew Jackson. Then there was the frog he trained to jump; Dan'l Webster was his name. Smiley won some money on him too. Then one day a stranger came along, challenged Dan'l's abilities, and in no time, a $40 bet was on. Smiley even obliged the stranger by catching him a frog for the contest, but the stranger secretly filled Dan'l with quail shot, so that he couldn't move, let alone jump, and Smiley was $40 poorer.

SUGGESTION

"The Celebrated Jumping Frog" is the perfect example of the tall tale, a type of humor associated with the American frontier. President Lincoln had an inexhaustible supply of tall tales and often used them to make a point. In a discussion of what makes them funny, students should discover that exaggeration and a "deadpan" delivery are essential to the tall tale, and that a tall tale usually involves a character who deserves his "comeuppance" (in this case, the overconfident Jim Smiley, who had bested many others).

ANSWER KEY

1. celebrated jumping frog

2. a man who loved to bet

3. a fighting bull pup

4. the man who bested Smiley

5. fictitious (?) friend of the narrator's friend

6. the storyteller

Name: _____

Date: _____

The Celebrated Jumping Frog of Calaveras County

Below are listed the names of several characters in the story. Identify each of them in the fewest possible words. (You shouldn't need more than six.)

1. _____

_____ Dan'l Webster

2. _____

_____ Jim Smiley

3. _____

_____ Andrew Jackson

4. _____

_____ the stranger in camp

5. _____

_____ Leonidas W. Smiley

6. _____

_____ Simon Wheeler

The Secret Life of Walter Mitty

James Thurber   *Easy*

SYNOPSIS

When the story opens, Walter Mitty is commanding a "Navy hydro-plane" until Mrs. Mitty brings him back to reality with a complaint about his driving. When he has left his wife at the hairdresser's he drops back into his dream world—this time as a world-famous surgeon facing a difficult case—but a parking-lot attendant disturbs his reverie. He has time for two more dreams and the errands his wife has assigned before he meets her at the hotel. As usual, she begins to scold, so he returns to his dream world, where he is always in command.

SUGGESTION

Students invariably enjoy this short story. If you ask them why Mitty creates a dream world, they should see for themselves that he does it because his real life allows him no dignity. They may then realize that the story has pathos as well as humor.

ANSWER KEY

1. He is always in command.

2. as far as driving is concerned, bumbling and inefficient

3. cold, domineering

4. She thinks he is ill and wants to take his temperature.

5. Neither husband nor wife is happy; Mitty escapes in dreams.

Name: _____

Date: _____

The Secret Life of Walter Mitty

Answering the following questions will help you to understand why Walter Mitty creates a dream world.

1. In Mitty's dreams, what kind of role does he invariably play?

   _____

   _____

2. What do the encounters with the traffic "cop," the parking-lot attendant, and the garageman in the wrecking car show about Mitty's real-life performance?

   _____

   _____

3. What two adjectives best describe Mrs. Mitty?

   _____

4. What is Mrs. Mitty's reaction to Walter's vague mumblings?

   _____

   _____

5. "The Secret Life of Walter Mitty" makes us smile, but thinking it over, you may decide that it is a sad story too. What makes it sad?

   _____

   _____

The Unicorn in the Garden

James Thurber

Easy

SYNOPSIS

As a man is eating his breakfast, he spies a unicorn eating roses in his garden. He wakes his wife to tell her, but she, unfriendly, says only, "The unicorn is a mythical beast." A second time the man goes upstairs to report on the unicorn. She tells him he is a "booby" and she will have him put into the "booby hatch." He says, "We'll see about that," and goes back to the now-empty garden for a nap. Meanwhile, the wife calls the police and a psychiatrist. They come, but when they hear what she has to say, they put her into a strait-jacket. When the husband denies all knowledge of a unicorn except that it is a mythical beast, they carry her off.

SUGGESTION

Students should be made aware that this short story fits the definition of a fable—a story with a moral (it is dangerous to take too much for granted!), often having an animal as one of the central characters. They can also have fun seeing how Thurber achieves his humorous effects, for example, the mock-serious report of the unicorn's presence and the unexpected turning of the tables on the unpleasant wife.

ANSWER KEY

1. the husband

2. We feel that she got what she deserved.

3. Answers will vary. The information makes the story funnier and more plausible.

4. Answers will vary. *Don't take too much for granted* is one possibility.

5. Yes. The wife told a strange story, and the husband seemed sane and logical.

Name: _____

Date: _____

The Unicorn in the Garden

1. Who is the sympathetic character in this story? (The one the author wants the reader to like.)

   _____

   _____

2. Why do we find it humorous that the sane wife is carted off in a strait-jacket?

   _____

   _____

3. Why do you think the author included exact information about what the unicorn was eating?

   _____

   _____

4. How would you restate the moral of the story, "Don't count your boobies until they are hatched"?

   _____

   _____

5. Were the police and the psychiatrist justified in their action? Explain.

   _____

   _____

   _____

The Death of Red Peril

Walter Edmonds   *Easy*

SYNOPSIS

The narrator's "pa" went from betting on horse races to betting on caterpillar races, caterpillars being more adaptable to life on canal boats. Red Peril was the best of the lot. As the family was riding home from church one Sunday, Pa had spotted him and recognized a winner. Pa trained him on the table, using the touch of a sharp pin to get him started. Once under way, there was no stopping him, but "he had a mortal fear of butter." That was almost his undoing once when a shifty lock tender tried to take advantage of Peril's phobia, but he went on to win lots of money for Pa, even his final race against the Horned Demon.

SUGGESTION

"The Death of Red Peril" is a good example of the tall tale, popular on the American frontier. Students who have read "The Celebrated Jumping Frog of Calaveras County" will see similarities in the two stories. Much of the humor comes from the mock-serious tone. The students should realize that reporting the caterpillar race in horse-racing terms and crediting Red Peril with quite remarkable intelligence catches the reader's interest even though he knows it's a spoof.

ANSWER KEY

1. B	6. C
2. H	7. D
3. I	8. E
4. F	9. A
5. G	10. J

Name: _____

Date: _____

The Death of Red Peril

Choose the appropriate word, phrase, or clause from Column A to complete each statement in Column B.

Column A

A. " . . . you've gone and dropped the butter."
B. "green and hairless as a newborn egg"
C. "one jab with a darning needle"
D. "jumped the ruts"
E. Paul Bunyan
F. "yeller chalk"
G. sly
H. Horned Demon
I. "sink his horns into the back end"
J. squeal

Column B

_____ 1. In his final race, Red Peril faced a creature that was _____ .

_____ 2. His name was the _____ of Rome.

_____ 3. A sneaky kind of racer, the first thing he did was _____ of Red Peril.

_____ 4. Red Peril had some bad moments when an unscrupulous lock tender laid out the course in _____ .

_____ 5. His name was Buscerek, and he could best be described as _____ .

_____ 6. The caterpillar men got their racers under way by giving them _____ .

_____ 7. When Pa saw Peril for the first time, he knew that caterpillar was a winner by the way he _____ .

_____ 8. One old man thought Red Peril must be descended from the caterpillars _____ used to race.

_____ 9. Ned spurred Peril to make the last run by shouting to him, _____ .

_____ 10. The thing that made Pa cry was Red Peril's final _____ .

       150 Great Short Stories

The Legend of Sleepy Hollow

Washington Irving   *Easy*

SYNOPSIS

In this ever-popular short story, Irving sets his scene carefully: the remote little village of Sleepy Hollow in which old legends and superstitions still flourish; the arrival of the schoolmaster, Ichabod Crane, a spectral figure himself and much given to musings on witchcraft and ghosts; the contrast between him and the powerfully built Brom Bones, his rival for the attention of Katrina Van Tassel, buxom daughter of a prosperous farmer. Everything seems peaceful, though, until the night of the "quilting frolic" at the Van Tassels', a party that begins well for Ichabod, but ends in his rejection by Katrina. The worst is yet to come; on his ride home, Ichabod is overtaken by the "headless horseman" of the legend and is never seen in Sleepy Hollow again.

SUGGESTION

It would be worthwhile to point out to the students that Irving uses tag-names to help to describe the characters: Ichabod *Crane* for the tall, gaunt schoolmaster; Brom *Bones* for Crane's physically powerful rival; *Sleepy Hollow* for the village where time seems to stand still. Ask the students to explain why even the horses' names are appropriate.

ANSWER KEY

1. Ichabod Crane
2. Sleepy Hollow
3. Baltus Van Tassel
4. Katrina Van Tassel
5. Gunpowder

6. Brom Bones
7. the Headless Horseman
8. Hans Van Ripper
9. Daredevil
10. the church bridge

Name: _____

Date: _____

The Legend of Sleepy Hollow

Washington Irving was very skillful in describing settings and characters. Your task here is to read the descriptions in Column A and match them with the people or places in Column B.

Column A

1. _____ " . . . tall, but exceedingly lank, with narrow shoulders, long arms and legs . . . "

2. _____ "A drowsy, dreamy influence seems to hang over the land . . . "

3. _____ " . . . an easy indulgent soul . . . loved his daughter better even than his pipe . . . "

4. _____ "blooming . . . plump as a partridge; ripe and melting and rosy-cheeked . . . "

5. _____ " . . . one eye had lost its pupil and was glaring and spectral; but the other had the gleam of a genuine devil . . . "

6. _____ " . . . broad-shouldered and double-jointed . . . Herculean frame and great powers of limb . . . "

7. _____ " . . . huge, misshapen, black and towering."

8. _____ "A choleric Old Dutchman" who had been "a furious rider"

8. _____ " . . . a creature . . . full of mettle and mischief . . . "

10. _____ At "a group of oaks and chestnuts matted thick with wild grapevines . . . "

Column B

Katrina Van Tassel   Daredevil
Brom Bones   the Headless Horseman
Hans Van Ripper   Sleepy Hollow
Baltus Van Tassel   Ichabod Crane
Gunpowder   the church bridge

The Revolt of the Evil Fairies

Ted Poston   *Easy*

SYNOPSIS

The biggest social event at Booker T. Washington Colored Grammar School is the annual presentation of *Prince Charming and Sleeping Beauty*. It is not by coincidence that the light-skinned children always play the lead parts and the good fairies. For this special occasion, the whites permit the school to use the Opera House and even come to sit in the first two rows for the performance. But this year, the narrator, doomed by his black skin to play the head evil fairy for the third year, livens up the evening by giving Prince Charming "a right to the chin," and when pandemonium follows, Sleeping Beauty heads for the wings.

SUGGESTION

Students should be made aware that although "The Revolt of the Evil Fairies" is a humorous story, it has tragic undertones. Since the story is brief, students could reread it, listing all the evidence of prejudice against the blacks in the school and the town.

ANSWER KEY

1. black; Kentucky
2. *Prince Charming and Sleeping Beauty*
3. light skin
4. head evil fairy
5. Sarah Williams
6. rapped; head; sword
7. sword; right to the chin
8. screaming
9. good fairy; fight
10. ran

Name: _____

Date: _____

The Revolt of the Evil Fairies

Fill in the blanks, using the fewest possible words, to complete each of the following sentences.

1. The setting of the story is a _____ grammar school

   in Hopkinsville, _____ .

2. Each year, the school presents a play, _____ .

3. To be chosen to play a lead part, a boy or girl has to have

   _____ .

4. The narrator never has had a chance to play the lead; instead, he is always cast as the

   _____ .

5. This year, he was especially eager to play the lead male role because he would have been cast

   opposite _____ .

6. Trouble started when the lead, Leonardius Wright, _____

   the narrator on the _____ with

   his _____ .

7. The narrator, having no _____ , gave Leonardius

   a _____ .

8. The audience thought they were seeing a new addition to the script until the teacher

   started _____ .

9. When Rat decided to beat up the nearest _____ , a

   general _____ followed.

10. At that point, the heroine _____ for the wings.

O'Halloran's Luck

Stephen Vincent Benét   *Easy*

SYNOPSIS

At the outset, Tim O'Halloran doesn't seem lucky. Because there is little for him at home in Ireland, he emigrates to America, following his sweetheart, Kitty Malone. But she, now a servant girl in Boston, is being courted by a horse-car conductor. Tim sees no chance for himself and takes a job laying track for the transcontinental railroad. Then a leprechaun comes into his life and gives him the stability of a man with responsibilities. The leprechaun also gives him some good advice that assures Tim's rapid advancement on the job and in his courtship of Kitty Malone. As for the leprechaun, having broken the spell cast on him by St. Patrick, he goes about his business, but never goes out of Tim's life entirely.

SUGGESTION

This humorous tale manages to combine fantasy and reality so effectively that the leprechaun becomes a believable character. Ask the students to point out concrete details about Rory's appearance and behavior that make him seem as human as Tim himself.

ANSWER KEY

1. former seat of English government in Ireland
2. site of July 1690 battle; forces of James II defeated by William of Orange
3. mythological Irish hero
4. Protestant followers of William of Orange; originally a secret society
5. seat of ancient Irish kings; also a religious site
6. generally, an Orangeman
7. terrible famine of the 1840's that brought many immigrants to America
8. boy; home-distilled whiskey
9. all fairies and spirits

O'Halloran's Luck

Although you can read and enjoy "O'Halloran's Luck" as a tall tale, it will have more significance if you recognize the historical references the author makes. Use a dictionary, a dictionary of mythology, or an Irish history to identify each of the following. Then reread the story to see if it has more meaning for you now.

1. _____ Dublin Castle (in Dublin, Ireland)

2. _____ Boyne Water (see River Boyne and Battle of the Boyne)

3. _____ Bones of Finn (Use a dictionary of mythology to find out who he was.)

4. _____ Orangeman (the street-car conductor) In Irish history, who are the Orangemen?

5. _____ Rock of Cashel (Try Irish historic sites.)

6. _____ Ulsterman (Connect this one with #4.)

7. _____ Famine (Check Irish history for an account of the mid-19th-century famine.)

8. _____ *Gossoon, potheen* (See dictionary)

9. _____ *Leprechaun, pooka, banshee* (Try the dictionary again.)

10. _____ For a special report, you might like to read about **THE BUILDING OF THE TRANSCONTINENTAL RAILROAD AND THE HARDSHIPS THE WORKERS SUFFERED.**

But I Didn't Do It

William Saroyan

Easy

SYNOPSIS

The narrator compares himself with his cousin Arak, who never gets into trouble at school and is invariably the "teacher's pet," while the narrator, argumentative and noisy, frequently ends up in the principal's office, getting the strap. Accused by his teacher of writing a poem which called her "ugly" and said she was in love with the principal (it was written by Arak), the narrator is sent to the office. He finds the principal's reaction strange—he is more pleased than angry, but the narrator's unwillingness to admit authorship earns him the usual punishment. A second poem and another trip to the office have an unexpected result for everyone, including the teacher, Miss Daffney.

SUGGESTION

This short story is a good one for teaching first-person point of view and its limitations. The story is told from the young boy's point of view. His concept of himself and of others may not be correct. Ask the students if they think his opinion of his own ability is accurate—for example, his explanation of why he hasn't been promoted. They might also speculate about what Miss Daffney's feelings for the pincipal were; did the boy read them correctly? As always, in a story told in the first person, the narrator is limited to describing his own reactions and others' reactions as he understands them.

ANSWER KEY

1. B	6. C	11. A
2. B	7. B	12. D
3. A	8. A	13. C
4. A	9. A	14. D
5. A	10. D	15. C

Name: _____

Date: _____

But I Didn't Do It

Match the descriptions in Column A with the characters in Column B to test your memory of the events in this story.

Column A

1. _____ Was "round-faced, dark, and elegant in manners"

2. _____ Had a smile that melted the teacher's heart

3. _____ Went to great lengths to prove he had done no wrong

4. _____ Spent a great deal of time in the principal's office

5. _____ Was the oldest pupil in his grade

6. _____ According to a poem, was "ugly" and in love with the principal

7. _____ Was the author of the poem in #6

8. _____ Got whacked on the knuckles

9. _____ Questioned the principal about his love life

10. _____ Thought the teacher was very attractive

11. _____ Protested, "I'm not going to carry love letters for you"

12. _____ Pretends to beat the narrator

13. _____ Catches the person in #12 pretending to beat the narrator

14. _____ Tries to explain the behavior in #13

15. _____ Didn't return to school the following year

Column B

A. the narrator
B. Arak
C. Miss Daffney
D. Mr. Derringer

The Fifty-first Dragon

Heywood Broun   *Moderate*

SYNOPSIS

Gawaine le Coeur-Hardy lacks spirit, and his instructors at knight school note his indifference in the jousting class. But the Headmaster, strong on "ethics and ideals," decides to train Gawaine to slay dragons. He gives the boy a course in both theory and practice. Finally, it is time to graduate from dummy dragons to the real thing. For that, the Headmaster gives Gawaine a magic word, *Rumplesnitz*. Armed with his battle axe and the charm, Gawaine slays forty-nine dragons. The fiftieth proves a bit hazardous; for a moment, Gawaine forgets the word, but manages to kill the dragon with the battle axe alone. Then the Headmaster makes the mistake of telling Gawaine that the word wasn't really magic, just a confidence-builder. After the next dragon encounter, nothing is left of Gawaine but his medals.

SUGGESTION

"The Fifty-first Dragon" is fun to read, but as humor often does, it makes a serious point. From discussion as to why Gawaine failed with the fifty-first dragon, students should be able to draw the conclusion that although he actually had inner strength, he had no faith in himself. Once the prop from without, *Rumplesnitz*, was removed, he could not perform.

ANSWER KEY

1. spirit
2. Answers will vary.
3. forgetfulness
4. cap
5. confidence
6. drinking
7. conceited
8. helpful
9. nerve
10. himself

Name: _____

Date: _____

The Fifty-first Dragon

One-word answers are all you need here.

1. _____ In his instructors' opinion, what did Gawaine lack?

2. _____ In your opinion, what adjective best describes his problem?

3. _____ What was Gawaine's "marvelously versatile gift" that made the course in theory of dragon-slaying difficult?

4. _____ Before facing a live dragon, Gawaine wanted an enchanted _____ .

5. _____ What the magic word *Rumplesnitz* actually gave Gawaine was _____ .

6. _____ After a number of successful dragon slayings, what bad habit did Gawaine acquire?

7. _____ His habit of wearing all his medals on his dragon hunts showed that he had also become _____ .

8. _____ When Gawaine couldn't remember the magic word, the old dragon tried to be _____ .

9. _____ When Gawaine discovered that *Rumplesnitz* really wasn't magic, he lost his _____ .

10. _____ Gawaine's real problem was that he had no confidence in _____ .

Gertrude the Governess: or Simple Seventeen

Stephen Leacock

Moderate

SYNOPSIS

In this humorous short story, Leacock has incorporated all the elements of the Gothic novel: the sweet and impoverished maiden (in this case, Gertrude); the scion of the aristocratic family who is supposed to marry money in order to save the estate (in this case, Lord Ronald); and the ruthless father (Lord Nosh), whose evil machinations long ago deprived the maiden's father of the estate that was rightfully his. Naturally, the two young people fall in love, marry, and live happily ever after, Lord Nosh having conveniently died in a hunting accident shortly after the wedding.

SUGGESTION

Leacock's treatment of an overused formula for third-rate novels is, of course, a parody, and students should become familiar with that term. But they can also have fun and, incidentally, engage in a bit of library and dictionary work, "verifying" some of the far-fetched details Leacock includes. For example, they might check what would be the approximate age of each addition to Nosham Taws—Elizabethan, Norman, Lancastrian, or Plantagenet. Some of the bird sounds need closer checking too.

ANSWER KEY

1. no—typically plaster and exposed beams

2. No, they would be at least 700 years old.

3. whirr; caw

4. No; Henry VII was Elizabeth's grandfather.

5. It would be pretty uncomfortable hanging down her back.

6. Rabies; a swoon or faint; a turning away from the audience

7. No—she'd be giving the equivalent of one pound sterling to each.

8. about 1½ inches

9. It made great sweeping circles around the horizon.

Name: _____

Date: _____

Gertrude the Governess: or Simple Seventeen

     To appreciate Leacock's humorous details, you are asked in this exercise to verify some of his seemingly serious statements. You'll need a dictionary and possibly a trip to the library for this one.

1. Nosham Taws is described in paragraph 4 of the story as an Elizabethan structure of warm red brick. Does that describe a typical Elizabethan house? Explain.

   _____

   _____

2. Is it probable that the Crusaders' geraniums would still be there? Explain.

   _____

   _____

3. What is a typical sound made by a partridge? A rook?

   _____

   _____

4. If the house is Elizabethan, is it likely that the avenue of trees was laid out by Henry VII? Explain.

   _____

   _____

5. Why is it unlikely that even Gertrude the Governess would carry a daguerreotype where she did? You probably don't need the dictionary for this one!

   _____

   _____

(continued)

Gertrude the Governess: or Simple Seventeen (continued)

6. Taking another look at the death of Gertrude's aunt, how is each of the following correctly defined?

   Hydrophobia _____

   Syncope _____

   Apostrophe _____

7. How about Gertrude's gifts to the servants when she arrived at Nosham Taws? Remember there was a "phalanx" of them, drawn up "seven deep," and she gave a sovereign to each. Is that the kind of "tip" a poor governess would be apt to give? Explain.

   _____

   _____

8. When the earl looked at Gertrude, he started as much as four centimeters. How far was that?

   _____

   _____

9. What was remarkable about the moon's behavior at Nosham Taws?

   _____

   _____

UNIT 3

A PORTRAIT GALLERY

Short-Story Characters You Won't Forget

UNIT 3

A PORTRAIT GALLERY
Short-Story Characters You Won't Forget 49

Big Blonde

Dorothy Parker

Easy

SYNOPSIS

Hazel, a "large, fair woman," worked as a model in the wholesale dress business. Because she was cheerful to the customers and flattered them, she was very popular. There she met, fell in love with, and married Herbie Morse, all within six weeks. At first, all went well, but Hazel no longer kept up her surface cheerfulness, and the gentle melancholy that was natural to her eventually drove Herbie away. After him came a succession of men who were all good to her but seemed to expect a cheerfulness that took more and more effort and alcohol. Finally, Hazel heard about veronal, and she made an unsuccessful suicide attempt. Once more, alcohol became her only key to oblivion.

SUGGESTION

Since "Big Blonde" is primarily a character sketch, ask the students to supply a chalkboard list of adjectives to describe Hazel physically and emotionally.

ANSWER KEY

1. many men
2. cheerful and flattering
3. melancholy
4. bored
5. marriage began to fail
6. "The Boys"
7. Ed
8. sad, cheerful
9. worries and complaints
10. Mrs. Miller
11. Nettie
12. always drunk

Name: _____

Date: _____

Big Blonde

Choose the appropriate word or phrase from Column A to complete each sentence in Column B.

Column A

melancholy	worries and complaints	marriage began to fail	Nettie
Ed	many men	sad, cheerful	"The Boys"
bored	Mrs. Miller	cheerful and flattering	always drunk

Column B

_____ 1. Hazel's job as a model in the wholsesale dress trade gives her a chance to meet _____ .

_____ 2. They like her because she is invariably _____ .

_____ 3. Underneath her facade, she is actually inclined to be _____ .

_____ 4. When she is no longer cheerful, Herbie becomes _____ with her.

_____ 5. She never cared much for drinking until her _____ .

_____ 6. It was through her neighbor, Mrs. Martin, that she met _____ .

_____ 7. _____ was Herbie's successor.

_____ 8. It puzzled Hazel that although other women could be _____ , she was expected to be always _____ .

_____ 9. Ed did not want to listen to her _____ .

_____ 10. _____ told Hazel about using veronal to put herself to sleep.

_____ 11. It was _____ who found Hazel after her overdose.

_____ 12. In the end, Hazel prays that she can remain _____ .

The Stout Gentleman

Washington Irving

Easy

SYNOPSIS

The narrator is spending a rainy November Sunday in a small English country inn and is feeling restless—there is little to amuse him and only the straw-strewn, mud-puddled inn yard for a view. Then he becomes interested in the servants' comings and goings, answering the numerous demands of another guest, whom they call "the stout gentleman." The narrator spends the rest of the day conjecturing about him. The next morning he gets a glimpse of the subject of his surmise as the stranger is stepping into the coach. "The skirts of a brown coat parted behind and gave me a full view of the broad disk of a pair of drab breeches . . . all I ever saw of the stout gentleman."

SUGGESTION

It was part of the genius of Washington Irving that he could fashion an entertaining tale from such "slight" material. "The Stout Gentleman" can serve as a "how-to" for a writing assignment. Ask the students to be sleuths, observing a stranger in a store or restaurant, on a bus, etc., and conjecture about him as Irving did, producing a character sketch for which they have no basis but their powers of observation and their imagination.

ANSWER KEY

1. eye showing undue amount of white
2. scullery maid
3. light, two-wheeled carriages
4. inn
5. a servant who shines shoes
6. stableboy
7. named or called
8. a magistrate
9. member of a liberal English political party
10. in an angry state
11. attic
12. hot wine drink

The Stout Gentleman

Because ''The Stout Gentleman'' was written in 1882, it is bound to contain words and references unfamiliar to you. Your task is to identify each of the following italicized words taken from the story. A dictionary will be all you need for most. One or two may send you to other reference books.

1. _____

_____ *wall-eyed* horse

2. _____

_____ kitchen *wench*

3. _____

_____ *gigs*

4. _____

_____ *hostel*

5. _____

_____ ''*Boots*''

6. _____

_____ *hostler*

(continued)

The Stout Gentleman (continued)

7. _____

_____ *ycleped* (old form of a common verb)

8. _____

_____ *alderman*

9. _____

_____ *Whig*

10. _____

_____ *dudgeon*

11. _____

_____ *garret*

12. _____

_____ *negus*

All the Years of Her Life

Morley Callaghan

Easy

SYNOPSIS

Alfred Higgins has been a drugstore clerk for six months when the owner, Sam Carr, accuses him of pilfering small items. At first, Alfred denies it, but the man's quiet voice frightens him, and he finally empties his pockets. Carr decides to phone Alfred's parents before calling the policeman. His father works nights, but his mother comes to get him out of trouble, as she has many times before. Carr is impressed with her composure and her dignity; they part friends. On the way home, Alfred tries to talk to her, but she brushes him off angrily. Then he sees her in the kitchen, sitting alone, old and beaten, and finally realizes what it cost her to face Sam Carr.

SUGGESTION

At first, the story appears to be about Alfred Higgins, but it is his mother who is the dominant character. As a worthwhile writing exercise, the students might use the title, "All the Years of Her Life," as the opening phrase of a sentence which summarizes Mrs. Higgins' experience.

ANSWER KEY

1. voice is soft and quiet

2. always in trouble

3. Maybe she can get him out of trouble.

4. calm, reasonable, dignified

5. likes her and wants to be reasonable

6. that he's a bad lot, always causing trouble

7. wants to say how proud he was of her in the drugstore

8. the effort it cost her to face Carr

Name: _____

Date: _____

All the Years of Her Life

Answer each question in one brief sentence.

1. What is different about the way Sam Carr speaks this night as he and Alfred are closing the drugstore?

    _____

    _____

2. What has been Alfred's work history?

    _____

    _____

3. What is Alfred thinking as Carr waits for his mother?

    _____

    _____

4. What is her attitude toward Mr. Carr?

    _____

    _____

5. What effect does it have on Mr. Carr?

    _____

    _____

(continued)

All the Years of Her Life (continued)

6. When Alfred tries to talk to his mother, what does she say?

   _____

   _____

7. Why does Alfred get up and go to the kitchen to talk to his mother again?

   _____

   _____

8. What does he finally realize?

   _____

   _____

Requiem for Bibul

Jack Ludwig

Easy

SYNOPSIS

The narrator recalls his senior year in Winnipeg High School in 1939. One of his classmates, Bibul, was responsible and serious while all the others were carefree and fun-loving. He had no time for extracurricular activities, sports, or girls, because when Bibul was not in the classroom, he was a fruit peddler, driving his ancient mare, Malkeh, bargaining in the wholesale market, and haggling with housewives, all to earn money for his education. Bibul intended to become a rabbi. Bibul did reach New York and begin his studies, but drowned one hot summer night in an unattended YMCA pool—he'd never had time to learn to swim.

SUGGESTION

"Requiem for Bibul" is a superb character sketch of an unusual person. Ask the students to supply adjectives describing Bibul's physical appearance and his outstanding qualities. Have one person record them on the chalkboard. If time allows, one student with artistic talent can then do a chalkboard sketch of Bibul, based on the adjectives.

ANSWER KEY

1. Winnipeg, Manitoba
2. 1939
3. student, fruit peddler
4. Malkeh
5. Bibul's name for his customers
6. to be a rabbi
7. lacks time and talent
8. Bibul's shopkeeper mother
9. drowns in YMCA pool
10. classmate of Bibul's

Name: _____

Date: _____

Requiem for Bibul

Answer each of the following questions in the fewest possible words.

1. _____ Where does the story take place?

2. _____ What year is it?

3. _____ What are the two occupations of the title character?

4. _____ What is his horse's name?

5. _____ Who are the *shnorrers*?

6. _____ What is Bibul's ambition?

7. _____ Why doesn't Bibul participate in extra-curricular activities?

8. _____ Who is known as either the "Golden Thumb" or the "Adder"?

9. _____ What finally happens to Bibul?

10. _____ Who tells the story?

Miss Brill

Katherine Mansfield

Moderate

SYNOPSIS

Miss Brill teaches English during the week and on four afternoons reads the newspaper to an "old invalid gentleman," but each Sunday she arrives at the Public Gardens to sit on a particular bench and watch other people. She would never admit that she is lonely, but the once-a-week activity is a high point, a time when she feels that she and all the other people in the park are players on the stage, each necessary to the production. Then two young lovers sit near her, and their carelessly critical remarks make her feel ridiculous and unwanted. She goes home deflated, with no heart for the small pleasures that have made her life bearable.

SUGGESTION

In "Miss Brill," very little happens except the lovers' conversation which devastates Miss Brill. Yet Mansfield holds the reader's interest by giving insight into the character of a lonely woman determined to see the best in her very narrow world. Ask the students to describe the main character, how she looks, thinks, and feels. They may need to be reminded that Miss Brill's reaction to others reveals a great deal about her. A good follow-up would be a writing assignment in which they attempt a character sketch too.

ANSWER KEY

1. A	6. E
2. F	7. D
3. I	8. C
4. G	9. B
5. H	

Name: _____

Date: _____

Miss Brill

Reread the passages in "Miss Brill" from which each of the following incidents or reactions is taken. Your job then is to match the incident or reaction with its significance. If you can do that correctly, you understand Miss Brill.

Incidents and Reactions

1. _____ Miss Brill's affection for her fur and her imagining that its eyes brighten after she has given it a good brushing

2. _____ Her noticing the band conductor's new coat

3. _____ Her disappointment that the elderly couple do not converse

4. _____ Her close observation of the children

5. _____ Her reaction to the woman who had dropped her violets and then threw them away after they were returned to her

6. _____ Her reaction to the woman in the ermine coat who meets the gentleman in grey

7. _____ Her musing that all the people in the park are actors in a play and her telling herself, "We understand"

8. _____ The fact that she doesn't stop at the baker's for a slice of honeycake

9. _____ The contrast between the way she puts her fur away and the way she had brought it out

Significance

A. Miss Brill needs something for which she can feel affection.

B. The girl's derogatory remark hurt Miss Brill deeply because she thinks of the fur as being alive and imagines it as being hurt too.

C. Temporarily, at least, she has lost her capacity for small pleasures and just wants to go home.

D. She needs to feel part of a group and believes they are as interested in her as she is in others.

E. Because she too has probably been disappointed by others and tried to hide it, she sees the woman's predicament and understands her attempt to put up a good front.

F. Everything about other people interests her because in that way she can feel part of the group.

G. For her they represent a part of life she has missed—having a family.

H. She is astonished that anyone could be so wasteful of a luxury and so indifferent to another's kindness.

I. She lives, vicariously, through others' lives. That is why she has become so skillful at eavesdropping.

Miss Cynthie

Rudolph Fisher

Easy

SYNOPSIS

Miss Cynthie has taken a two-day journey north to New York to visit her grandson David; she wants to see if he has amounted to "sump'n." David meets her train. He is obviously prosperous, but tells Miss Cynthie she will have to wait a bit to find out what his work is. The next evening, he takes her to the theater (a place synonymous with sin in her mind), but the real shock comes when she discovers her grandson is the star of the show. She is bitterly disappointed until she realizes how much the audience appreciates David, and when he points her out as his inspiration, her pride and love are boundless.

SUGGESTION

"Miss Cynthie" is an excellent example of a short story in which the author acquaints the reader with a character, not by telling what the person is like, but by showing that person's reactions and others' reactions to him or her. Ask the students how Miss Cynthie's conversation with the black porter, her reaction to Harlem, and her reaction to the theater show the reader what kind of person she is.

ANSWER KEY

1. 70
2. first time more than 50 miles from home
3. to visit her grandson
4. be a preacher, a doctor, or at least an undertaker
5. that he might be making money illegally
6. She liked it.
7. churches
8. the song she sings
9. asks God's forgiveness
10. his dancing to the tune of the old song she taught him

Name: _____

Date: _____

Miss Cynthie

Answer the following question in as few words as possible.

_____ 1. How old is Miss Cynthie?

_____ 2. How much has she traveled?

_____ 3. Why has she come to New York?

_____ 4. What advice did she give David before he left home?

_____ 5. When she sees David's expensive car, what worries her?

_____ 6. What was her reaction to David's passing all the other cars?

_____ 7. When David shows her Harlem's theater, she is unimpressed, but what buildings do impress her?

_____ 8. What indication is there that Miss Cynthie likes music and fun?

_____ 9. When she realizes that they are going to the theater that evening, what is her reaction?

_____ 10. What action of David's wins over Miss Cynthie and makes her realize the audience is not sinful, but childlike in their enjoyment of the show?

Jug of Silver

Truman Capote

Easy

SYNOPSIS

Marshall's *Valhalla*, the only drugstore in a small southern town, does a thriving business until a stranger opens an up-to-date pharmacy across the square. But Mr. Marshall devises a scheme to drive out his upstart competitor: For each 25¢ purchase, customers get a chance to guess how many nickels and dimes a gallon wine jug on the counter contains. The winner will take all on Christmas Eve! Appleseed, a shabby eight-year-old from a hardscrabble farm three miles out of town, comes daily to stare at the jug and "count" the money. Finally, he makes his guess: $77.35. To the astonishment of the townspeople who gather for the Christmas Eve drawing, the jug does contain that amount.

SUGGESTION

Students will have no difficulty with the suspenseful plot, but to increase their awareness of Capote's beautiful evoked, nostalgic setting, ask them to compare and contrast this little Southern town with their own at Christmastime.

ANSWER KEY

1. H	6. E	11. B
2. E	7. A	12. G
3. C	8. C	13. F
4. E	9. A	14. B
5. H	10. D	15. E

Jug of Silver

To discover whether or not you are well acquainted with the characters in "Jug of Silver," match the name of the person in Column B with the description in Column A. Any name may be used more than once.

Column A

1. _____ Was the town drunk

2. _____ Was only eight but claimed to be twelve

3. _____ Found a way to get rid of his rival

4. _____ Interested in winning the money for someone else's sake

5. _____ Played Santa Claus

6. _____ Was born with a caul

7. _____ Wanted to be in the movies

8. _____ Owned the *Valhalla*

9. _____ Had poor teeth

10. _____ Opened a store in competition with the *Valhalla*

11. _____ Was an Egyptian and would-be writer

12. _____ Was the story's narrator

13. _____ Went mad and claimed to have discovered oil

14. _____ Hatched a plot with Mr. Marshall

15. _____ Had strong faith in his own abilities

Column B

A. Middy

B. Hamurabi

C. Mr. Ed Marshall

D. Rufus McPherson

E. Appleseed

F. Station Master Tully

G. Ed Marshall's nephew

H. Mr. R.C. Judkins

Free Joe and the Rest of the World

Joel Chandler Harris

Easy

SYNOPSIS

About 1840, a stranger, Major Frampton, came to the little town of Hillsborough, Georgia. A gambler, Frampton lost everything he owned playing cards with a local man, Judge Wellington. All Frampton had held back was his manservant, Joe. Having signed the papers giving Joe his freedom, Frampton committed suicide. Scorned by other blacks and held in suspicion by the whites, Free Joe remained in Hillsborough because his wife Lucinda now belonged to Judge Wellington. When Wellington died, his half-brother, a mean man named Calderwood, inherited his estate. Joe was no longer permitted to visit Lucinda, but for a while they managed to rendezvous under a poplar tree off Calderwood's land. There, Joe was eventually found dead.

SUGGESTION

This is a good story to demonstrate the term *pathos* to the students. Harris evokes the reader's pity and compassion for Joe, who could not find acceptance with blacks or whites, but who was grateful even to subsist.

ANSWER KEY

1. F	6. G	11. F
2. C	7. H	12. B
3. E	8. G	13. F
4. B	9. E	14. A
5. D	10. A	15. B

Free Joe and the Rest of the World

Match the descriptions in Column A with the characters in Column B.

Column A

1. _____ Joe's faithful dog

2. _____ The winner in a big card game

3. _____ Free Joe's wife

4. _____ A gambler who lost

5. _____ A mean and spiteful man

6. _____ A fortune-teller

7. _____ A poor white with a palsied arm and hand

8. _____ Occasionally gave Joe coffee

9. _____ Was sent away by that mean man

10. _____ Was found dead under a poplar tree

11. _____ Was killed by the mean man's hounds

12. _____ Set Joe free

13. _____ Would run and fetch Joe's wife

14. _____ Was not accepted by whites or blacks

15. _____ Thought it would be easy to make money in Hillsborough because the people were innocent

Column B

A. Free Joe

B. Major Frampton

C. Judge Wellington

D. Calderwood

E. Lucinda

F. Little Dan

G. Miss Becky Staley

H. Micajah Staley

María Concepción

Katherine Anne Porter

Moderate

SYNOPSIS

María Concepción, a happily married young Mexican woman, is religious, energetic, and shrewd. Her husband Juan works for Givens, the archaeologist excavating an ancient site. When María discovers that Juan is unfaithful, everything changes. He joins the army, taking his new love along. Left alone, María has her baby. It dies soon after birth, and María withdraws from her neighbors, making the church her only consolation. Then Juan and his María Rosa return. Juan is jailed as a deserter, but Givens has him released. That very day, María Rosa has his baby, but Juan spends his time getting drunk. He returns home in a stupor to sleep, but wakes up to the realization that María Concepción has murdered her rival. He and the other villagers outwit the gendarmes. María Concepción is free to take María Rosa's baby and go back home with her husband.

SUGGESTION

Aside from her remarkable character sketch of María Concepción, Porter offers her readers a glimpse of a primitive society with its own mores. Students might discuss the role of women and men in that society, the part superstition played in the people's lives, and the people's concept of justice.

ANSWER KEY

1. B	6. F	11. A	16. A
2. D	7. A	12. A	17. C
3. A	8. B	13. E	18. D
4. E	9. C	14. E	19. A and C
5. B	10. C	15. C	20. B

Reading Quiz:

Another Look at the Characters in the Story

Name: _____

Date: _____

María Concepción

If you can match the words or phrases in Column A with the characters in Column B, you remember the characters in the story as Katharine Anne Porter described them.

Column A

1. _____ The beekeeper
2. _____ The medicine woman
3. _____ Juan's wife
4. _____ Juan's employer
5. _____ Juan's girlfriend
6. _____ The thinker and peacemaker
7. _____ A proud woman
8. _____ Shy and pretty
9. _____ Swaggering
10. _____ Unfaithful
11. _____ Hardworking
12. _____ Religious
13. _____ The archaeologist
14. _____ Juan's rescuer
15. _____ A deserter
16. _____ A shrewd businesswoman
17. _____ Resourceful
18. _____ A believer in evil spirits
19. _____ Church-married (two letters)
20. _____ The victim of revenge

Column B

A. María Concepción

B. María Rosa

C. Juan Villegas

D. Lupe

E. Givens

F. Soledad

Wash

William Faulkner

Moderate

SYNOPSIS

After the Civil War, a plantation owner, Colonel Sutpen, is reduced to running a store for the blacks and poor whites, but still has one devoted follower. "Poor white trash," Wash lives with his granddaughter in a broken-down cabin on the colonel's land and drinks with him regularly, but never forgets his place. When the colonel shows some interest in the granddaughter, Wash "knows" he will act responsibly, brave gentleman that he is. But when the girl gives birth, Sutpen comes, looks at the baby, and tells her, "Too bad you're not a mare. Then I could give you a decent stall in the stable." Only then does Wash realize his idol has feet of clay, and his revenge is terrible.

SUGGESTION

"Wash" is representative of Faulkner's fiction in two ways, and both are worth calling to the students' attention. First, subject matter: The arrogant, aristocratic and degenerate Sutpen and his good-for-nothing hanger-on, Wash, are both Southern types that he regularly writes about. Second, style: The second sentence in the first paragraph, more than 60 words long and difficult in structure, is a good example of Faulkner's prose.

ANSWER KEY

1. Wash's granddaughter, when Wash comes in after killing Sutpen
2. Wash, when the posse comes to get him
3. Wash, when he is about to kill his granddaughter before surrendering
4. Sutpen, to the granddaughter, just after their child is born
5. Wash, whenever Sutpen needs cheering up
6. Wash, to Sutpen, talking about the granddaughter

Name: _____

Date: _____

Wash

In this exercise, you are to identify the speaker and explain briefly when he or she made that speech.

1. "I want a sup of water. I been laying here wanting a sup of water a long time, but nobody care enough to pay me no mind."

   _____

   _____

2. "I'm here. That you, Major?"

   _____

   _____

3. "Hit won't need no light, honey. Hit won't take but a minute."

   _____

   _____

4. "Too bad you're not a mare. Then I could give you a decent stall in the stable."

   _____

   _____

5. "We ain't whupped yet, air we? Me and you kin do hit."

   _____

   _____

6. "I ain't afraid because you air brave . . . I know that whatever you handle or tech . . . that you will make hit right."

   _____

   _____

UNIT 4

SURVIVAL ═══════════════════

Stories of Adventure and Danger in the Outdoors

UNIT 4

SURVIVAL

Stories of Adventure and Danger in the Outdoors 73

To Build a Fire

Jack London

Easy

SYNOPSIS

The Yukon Trail is grey, sunless, and cold (75° below zero) as a man and his dog head toward camp on Henderson Creek, a day's trek away. A tenderfoot, the man has been warned that no one should travel alone in this country when the temperature dips below –50°, but he is feeling quite confident until he breaks through snow, softened by a hidden spring, and soaks his clothing halfway to his knees. His attempt to build a fire and dry out almost succeeds, but snow dropping from a nearby spruce puts out the flame, and his attempt to rekindle it fails. In a panic, he runs until he collapses. The dog trots off toward camp and other "fire providers."

SUGGESTION

You can use "To Build a Fire" effectively to demonstrate the difference between theme (the controlling idea) and plot (what happens next). You might point out that one idea the author puts forth in this story is "survival of the fittest"; the man lacks imagination, London tells us, and perhaps that is his undoing. The dog survives. Why? In a discussion, students should be able to discover other themes in which "To Build a Fire."

ANSWER KEY

1. Yukon Territory
2. –75°
3. imagination
4. traveling alone
5. the danger of hidden springs
6. master and servant
7. builds it under a tree
8. His hands are numb.
9. The man acts strangely.
10. trots off toward camp and other "fire providers"

Name: _____

Date: _____

To Build a Fire

Fill in the blanks with the fewest possible words.

1. _____ Where does the action take place? (proper name)

2. _____ How cold is it?

3. _____ What does the author say is lacking in the man's make-up?

4. _____ What mistake has he already made when the story begins?

5. _____ What makes him wary as he trudges through the snow?

6. _____ What is the relationship between the man and dog?

7. _____ What mistake does the man make in building the first fire?

8. _____ Why does he have so much difficulty building the second fire?

9. _____ Why is the dog suspicious?

10. _____ When the man collapses for the final time, what does the dog do?

Matches
Viola Paradise

Easy

SYNOPSIS

Two young women arrive by auto-stage at the tar paper shanty which is to be their homestead in the Great West. Because another passenger has traveled 100 miles to get a doctor for his seriously ill wife and is understandably impatient, the stage stops only long enough to unload the girls' gear. To ward off the penetrating cold, they decide to light a fire, but the matches are missing. Thus begins their ten-day ordeal marooned in a lonely world of snow. Their resourcefulness keeps them alive. Finally, when they are close to death, they are found and saved by the young doctor who had been their stage companion.

SUGGESTION

"Matches" makes use of coincidence: the young doctor happens to be aboard the stage with the girls; the box of soap and box of matches happen to be same size so that the storekeeper makes a terrible mistake; the sheep happens to come to the door of the shanty; the doctor happens to be the one to find the girls and, because of his skill, can save their lives. Students should be made aware that coincidence is a useful device in fiction, but that too much coincidence detracts from a story. Have them decide whether or not it is overused in this short story.

ANSWER KEY

1. Little Willie
2. Dr. Calhoun
3. Louise Elmhurst
4. the fat man
5. Lee Dodd

6. Frances Stead
7. Louise Elmhurst
8. Frances Stead
9. Dr. Calhoun
10. Lee Dodd

Name: _____

Date: _____

Matches

If you read closely, you know that each of the following descriptions could fit only one character. You are asked to match character and description.

Characters

Lee Dodd

Frances Stead

Dr. Calhoun

Louise Elmhurst

the fat man

Little Willie

Descriptions

1. _____ He was the six-foot driver.

2. _____ He was romantically interested in Frances.

3. _____ She was very much in love and saw most events as raw material for stories.

4. _____ He was terribly worried about his wife and worried that bad weather might delay the stage.

5. _____ He thought that a homestead in the Great West was no place for women in the winter.

6. _____ She was strong and resourceful.

7. _____ She was enthusiastic and affectionate, but not as capable as her companion.

8. _____ She was the one who had thought homesteading would be an interesting thing to do.

9. _____ He was so uneasy about the girls that he made a difficult journey on horseback through the snow.

10. _____ He had left the shanty in good condition for its new tenants, but he had misgivings.

The Open Boat

Stephen Crane

Moderate

SYNOPSIS

Off the Florida coast, four men are in an open boat, survivors of the steamer *Commodore*, which has sunk. The injured captain can only direct the men. The cook cannot row. Somehow, the other two, the oiler and the newspaper correspondent, keep the boat from swamping and keep it on course. Once, they get close enough to shore to see people gaily waving, unaware that the men in the boat are fighting for their lives. For a while, a shark circles. Finally, the men take a chance on bringing the boat in. The oiler drowns, but with the help of one rescuer, the others make it.

SUGGESTION

In this famous short story, the correspondent voices Crane's theme, that man, important only to himself, pits his puny strength against the powerful, indifferent forces of nature. To test students' understanding of "The Open Boat," ask them to write a single sentence which states the main idea of the story. It might be advisable to caution them that they are not summarizing what happens, but the *significance* of what happens.

ANSWER KEY

1. Loss of his ship is always a terrible blow to the captain.

2. For morale's sake, they need to believe it is near.

3. Facing almost certain death, they are angry that land is so close, as if the Fates were torturing them.

4. It is indifferent; one person matters very little.

5. He seemed the strongest and best equipped to survive.

The Open Boat

Answer each of the questions in one carefully worded sentence.

1. Why is the captain even more dejected than the other men?

   _____

   _____

   _____

2. Even though the correspondent cannot see the lighthouse, why are the other crew members so certain that they see it?

   _____

   _____

   _____

3. Carne says that the men felt "rage." What made them angry?

   _____

   _____

   _____

4. When the others are asleep and the shark is circling, what are the correspondent's thoughts about nature?

   _____

   _____

   _____

5. What is ironic about the oiler's being the one who died?

   _____

   _____

   _____

The Rescuers

David Walker

SYNOPSIS

A writer, Douglas, has spent the fall and winter alone in a house on a remote Scottish hillside and has watched the river which winds through the meadow below him. On this stormy spring evening, his neighbor's sheep are still grazing in the meadow, although the river is swollen and rising. Late the same night, the neighbor and his daughter come to ask Douglas's help in rescuing the sheep. They get all but two onto safe ground before the river breaks over its banks, stranding Douglas. After a night that tests Douglas's strength and courage, the farmer and his daughter manage to rescue him.

SUGGESTION

Although this is an exciting adventure story, it is also a story in which setting is extremely important. So that the students will be aware of how carefully the author sets the scene, ask them to list words or phrases that describe the look and action of the river and the sound of the wind. (For example, "grey and shabby sullenness," "surged," and "buffeting.")

ANSWER KEY

1. Reid's daughter
2. wind
3. river
4. wind
5. river
6. Reid
7. Douglas
8. Reid
9. Reid's daughter
10. Douglas
11. Reid
12. Douglas to himself
13. Reid
14. Reid
15. Reid's daughter

The Rescuers

"The Rescuers" has only three characters:

> the writer, Douglas
> the farmer, Reid
> Reid's daughter

But in a sense, the river and the wind are also "characters," for the author describes them and their actions. Each of the following words or phrases describes one of the three people or one of the two forces of nature. In the space provided, show who or what is being described.

1. _____ Big, red-headed, silent, strong

2. _____ Screaming, blustering

3. _____ Quiet, impetuous, vicious

4. _____ Buffeting and booming

5. _____ Fickle, sometimes furious

6. _____ Tall, dark, taciturn

7. _____ Frightened but resourceful

In the story, who made each of the following remarks? (They are not in order.)

8. _____ "Do as I tell ye."

9. _____ "I'm coming too."

10. _____ "Come in out of that wild night."

11. _____ "The waves are lapping on the brink."

12. _____ "You bloody coward."

13. _____ "The flood is up, and the sheep are still on the haugh."

14. _____ "Run for yon tree . . . We'll get the boat."

15. _____ "We had to wait for the day, you're not hurt?"

Flame on the Frontier

Dorothy Johnson

Easy

SYNOPSIS

In a Sioux raid on a settler's cabin, the husband and two grown sons are killed. The mother hides her retarded son and the baby, then comes out of hiding herself to distract the Indians from her children. She is taken by the Indians, but escapes, is eventually reunited with her two children, and remarries. When the raid begins, her two daughters, Mary Amanda and little Sarah, are at the spring and are taken by the Indians. Sarah's courage so impresses the braves that her sister's life is spared. Although Mary Amanda is reluctant to adopt the Indian way of life, she eventually marries a brave, and it is Sarah who returns to the white man's world, but she never forgets her Indian friends.

SUGGESTION

This short story contrasts the American Indians' lifestyle with the whites' and gives insights on the status of women in both societies. Ask the students to find and list the contrasts in such areas as courtship, distribution of work, and treatment of the children.

ANSWER KEY

1. D	11. J
2. G	10. L
3. K	11. B
4. E	12. A
5. C	13. M
6. C, F	14. M
7. H	15. N
8. I	

Flame on the Frontier

In Column A below are several incomplete statements. Choose the proper word
or phrase from Column B to complete each of them.

Column A

_____ 1. That Sunday afternoon, the Harris family was alerted by _____ that the Indians were about
to attack.

_____ 2. Mrs. Harris's warning to her retarded son was not to _____ until the Indians killed him.

_____ 3. Hannah Harris _____ to save her two sons.

_____ 4. In later years, Johnny remembered that one terrible afternoon when his mother _____ .

_____ 5. The Indians might have killed Mary Amanda because she was too weak to walk if _____ had
not intervened.

_____ 6. In the Indian camp, _____ was a great favorite and was renamed_____because she chattered.

_____ 7. _____ saw the Indian ways as contemptible and had trouble adjusting.

_____ 8. The brave that Mary Amanda eventually chose for a husband was _____ .

_____ 9. Hannah Harris's second husband _____ wanted to go on the expedition to bring the girls
back to the white settlement, but his wife dissuaded him.

_____ 10. Mary Amanda's husband assumed that she would return to her own people and decided
to _____ .

_____ 11. Big Moon brought fine gifts to Mary Amanda's lodge, gifts intended as her _____ .

_____ 12. Back with the whites, Sarah eventually married _____ .

_____ 13. _____ , a Sioux, once visited Sarah to be sure she was happy and well provided for.

_____ 14. When her husband came in, Sarah pretended not to know _____ because she was afraid her
husband would try to pick a fight with him.

_____ 15. Sarah lived to see one of her sons _____ .

Column B

A. the blacksmith

B. ransom

C. Sarah

D. Mary Amanda's scream

E. put more trust in him than
in God

F. Bluejay

G. let go of the baby

H. Mary Amanda

I. Snow Mountain

J. Link Bartlett

K. risked her own life

L. go away

M. Horse Ears

N. elected to the state
legislature

The Erne from the Coast

T.O. Beachcroft

Easy

SYNOPSIS

At thirteen, Harry is still so immature that his farmer father has little patience with him. But Harry is sent to the shepherd's hut to tend the sheep while the old shepherd is away. An erne, a huge, hawklike bird, steals one of the lambs, and when Harry goes back to the farm to tell his father, the father doesn't believe his story and beats him. Next morning, the bird strikes again. The sheep dog tries to drive him off, but the bird kills him. Harry is determined to avenge the dog's death and prove himself. He succeeds, after a bloody battle, and carries the dead bird home to show his father that he did not lie and that he can be trusted to act responsibly.

SUGGESTION

"The Erne from the Coast" is an exciting adventure story, but it is also a story that gives a glimpse of a way of life different from what most students will have experienced. Dialect, word choices, and descriptions create an unfamiliar setting. In discussion, ask the students how Mr. Thorburn's treatment of Harry and his expectations of what the boy should be able to do differ from their own parents' treatment and expectations.

ANSWER KEY

1. more maturity
2. read
3. "knows a thing or two"
4. broke his wrist
5. make himself useful
6. come to harm
7. afraid
8. money
9. "That's a lie."
10. brought back the eagle
11. to avenge Tassie and prove himself to his father
12. stay alive
13. happier
14. erne
15. apologize

The Erne from the Coast

Complete the following statements, using the number of words suggested in parentheses.

_____ 1. Mr. Thorburn is sometimes impatient with Harry because he expects the boy to behave _____ . (2 words)

_____ 2. Harry is slightly scornful of the shepherd because the old man cannot _____ . (1 word)

_____ 3. Mr. Thorburn tells his son tartly that Michael _____ that Harry doesn't. (5 words)

_____ 4. Mr. Thorburn only gave Harry the responsibility of tending the sheep because Michael's nephew, Bob, fell and _____ . (3 words)

_____ 5. Mr. Thorburn tells the boy that tending the sheep will be a chance for him to _____ . (3 words)

_____ 6. Harry's mother reassures him that he can't _____ at the shepherd's hut. (3 words)

_____ 7. Both the dog and Harry run at the eagle, but both are _____ . (1 word)

_____ 8. One reason that Mr. Thorburn was in a bad mood when Harry returned to the farm had to do with _____ . (1 word)

(continued)

The Erne from the Coast (continued)

_____ 9. When Harry told the story of the eagle and the lamb, his father said angrily, _____ . (3 words)

_____ 10. As Harry walked out of the farmyard, his father called after him that he would believe Harry's story only if he _____ . (4 words)

_____ 11. Harry faced up to the eagle for two reasons: _____ . (9 words)

_____ 12. Before the encounter with the eagle was over, Harry was fighting just to _____ . (2 words)

_____ 13. Back home once more, even though he was in pain, Harry was _____ than he had ever been before. (1 word)

_____ 14. It was old Michael, with his practical knowledge and experience, who identified the bird as an _____ . (1 word)

_____ 15. Harry had thought his father might eventually _____ for the beating, but he did not. (1 word)

Hook

Walter Van Tilburg Clark

Moderate

SYNOPSIS

Hook, pushed early from the nest by his hawk parents and unable to fly, learns survival in a harsh environment. Almost simultaneously, he masters flight and satisfies his lust to kill. Reaching full maturity, he mates briefly and then returns to hunting alone. Ruthlessly, he destroys any hawk who invades his territory, but gets a few injuries in the process. Then a blast from a farmer's shotgun destroys one of Hook's wings, and once more he must forage on the ground. Seeing his helplessness, the gulls attack and peck out one of his eyes. Now he is concerned only with survival, but a prolonged drought makes food so scarce that he is driven to entering the farmer's chicken coop. When the dog hears the hens' commotion, he alerts the family. They watch Hook's valiant last stand, but the dog, encouraged by his master, finally kills Hook.

SUGGESTION

During a discussion of this story, you might want to introduce the critical term *pathetic fallacy*, defined as crediting the elements of the natural world with the "moods and passions of a human being." Students can decide whether or not Clark goes beyond the limits of credibility when he describes Hook's feelings and reactions.

ANSWER KEY

1. to fly effortlessly, to kill, and to mate

2. courageous

3. Answers will vary.

4. his pent-up fury at his helplessness; also, hens presented a challenge because of their size

5. Answers will vary.

Hook

1. What three great urges motivated Hook?

   _____

   _____

   _____

2. What adjective best describes him?

   _____

3. You have heard the term "survival of the fittest." Apply it specifically to an event in Hook's life.

   _____

   _____

   _____

4. Usually, animals kill to feed themselves and survive. How do you account for Hook's killing hen after hen in the coop?

   _____

   _____

   _____

5. How did you react to the farmer's and his son's behavior during Hook's last battle?

   _____

   _____

   _____

Mountain Medicine

A.B. Guthrie Jr.

Easy

SYNOPSIS

Two beaver trappers are making their rounds. The "greenhorn," Bill Potter, is skeptical of the old timer, John Clell, who insists that Indians are nearby and that they should lie low. Potter taunts Clell into continuing their canoe journey downriver. When Indians appear out of nowhere, Potter shows fear and stupidly fires his gun. The Indians then pick him off with a shower of arrows. Clell, who is captured, tries to "make medicine" that will secure his release, but the chief decides he will be freed only if he can outrun the braves and reach the nearest fort. Clell, who eludes his pursuers by hiding in a beaver house, finally reaches the fort days later, but he never wants to trap beavers again.

SUGGESTION

John Clell is rendered in the tradition of the "frontier hero" who has appeared in our literature again and again, from the novels of James Fenimore Cooper to the modern western stories of Louis L'Amour. Students should be able to identify the characteristics such heroes have in common; for example, they are strong, silent, solitary, resourceful, courageous, and in tune with nature.

ANSWER KEY

1. greenhorn
2. buffalo
3. fires his gun
4. Clell's gun
5. shooting an eagle, releasing the secret catch

6. run
7. hiding in a beaver lodge
8. showering him with arrows
9. several days
10. would never trap beaver again

Name: _____

Date: _____

Mountain Medicine

Complete the following sentences, using the writing spaces at the left.

_____ 1. Bill Potter is a _____ who has not been in the West very long.

_____ 2. When Clell thinks he hears Indians, Potter says the noise is caused by _____ .

_____ 3. Potter signs his own death warrant when he _____ .

_____ 4. Mule Ear is the name of _____ .

_____ 5. Clell makes medicine by _____ and _____ on his gun.

_____ 6. The chief decides to let Clell _____ for his freedom.

_____ 7. Clell escapes the Indians by _____ .

_____ 8. The Indians kill Potter by _____ .

_____ 9. It takes Clell _____ to reach the fort.

_____ 10. Clell didn't tell the other white men about hiding in a beaver lodge, but he _____ .

When Twilight Falls on the Stump Lots

Sir Charles G.D. Roberts

Easy

SYNOPSIS

In a stump lot at the edge of the forest, a cow has just given birth to her first calf. Now the little one struggles to its feet to begin nursing. Nearby but hidden, a she-bear, thin from hibernation, watches the two and begins edging closer, made bold enough by hunger to attack the cow and her newborn. But the cow gets the bear's scent and charges. A fierce battle ensues with the cow emerging the victor. The bear slinks back toward her den where two cubs wait, but dies before reaching it. The cubs fall victim to hungry foxes, but the cow and calf are found the next morning and taken back to safety so that in a few weeks the calf can be slaughtered.

SUGGESTION

Students should be encouraged to find parallels in this story: the cow's love for the calf and the bear's for her cubs; the struggle for survival and concern for their young which motivate the cow and the bear; and, of course, its futility, since both cubs and calf are killed.

ANSWER KEY

1. stump lot
2. in hibernation
3. steal lambs
4. cow
5. charges bravely

6. off balance
7. cow
8. den
9. foxes
10. slaughtered

Reading Quiz:

Mother Love

Name: _____

Date: _____

When Twilight Falls on the Stump Lots

Two or three words are sufficient to answer each of the following.

_____ 1. The bear can creep close to the cow without being seen because the cow has given birth in a _____ .

_____ 2. The bear is thin and hungry because it has been _____ .

_____ 3. Because most of her usual forage is not available, the bear has been forced recently to _____ for food so that she will be able to nurse her cubs.

_____ 4. Only desperation would make the bear bold enough to attack a _____ .

_____ 5. Because of a wind shift, the cow gets warning that the bear is near and _____ .

_____ 6. The bear is at a disadvantage because she is momentarily _____ .

_____ 7. In the battle, the _____ is the victor.

_____ 8. The bear tries unsuccessfully to reach her _____ .

_____ 9. Her cubs eventually are killed by _____ .

_____ 10. The calf eventually is _____ .

Early Marriage

Conrad Richter

Easy

SYNOPSIS

Asa Putnam's trading post is a tiny speck in the vast Santa Ana Plain. He is scheduled to escort his sixteen-year-old daughter, Nancy Belle, to meet her bridegroom at Gunstock, a five-day wagon journey away. But the Apaches are on the warpath, and no one is traveling, including the man who was to be Asa's relief at the trading post. Reluctantly, Asa lets his two children, Nancy Belle and her fifteen-year-old brother, start out for the Rio Grande. Fear is ever-present, and they have various mishaps, including a dangerous crossing of the rain-swollen river, but they encounter no Indians, and the wedding takes place on schedule.

SUGGESTION

"Early Marriage" has all the elements of the typical "western story": the threat of Indians; the wagon journey; and the various hazards of the trail. But it is, more significantly, a story of personal courage and resourcefulness. Ask the students to list, on the chalkboard or orally, the ways in which the two young people showed those qualities.

ANSWER KEY

1. suspects he may have encountered Indians
2. She was a woman of refinement whose family didn't approve of the place her husband brought her to.
3. says she can get to Gunstock all right
4. It will be easier for both of them if they don't put their fear of Indians into words.
5. Apparently, Asa told his son to take care of Nancy Belle.
6. talks aloud to herself about her childhood
7. Nancy Belle drives all night.
8. her trousseau
9. She says her father couldn't come, so Rife brought her.

94

Name: _____

Date: _____

Early Marriage

Answer each of the following questions as briefly as possible.

1. Why do you think Asa Putnam is not hopeful that Uncle Gideon may still arrive to take over the post?

   _____

   _____

2. What did you gather was the difference between Asa's background and his wife's?

   _____

   _____

3. What does Nancy Belle say that draws her father's secret admiration?

   _____

   _____

4. Why doesn't Rife tell Nancy Belle what he and the bearded man on the trail talked about?

   _____

   _____

5. Nancy Belle, the older, says that she will ride over and check the situation at Martin Cross's cabin. Why doesn't Rife let her?

   _____

   _____

(continued)

           150 Great Short Stories

Early Marriage (continued)

6. What does Nancy Belle do to keep calm while the coyotes are circling the wagon?

   _____

   _____

7. How do they make up the time lost rounding up the horses?

   _____

   _____

8. What is Nancy Belle thinking of when the river water comes into the wagon?

   _____

   _____

9. When Nancy Belle meets Stephen and the others, how does she show her brother her appreciation for what he has done?

   _____

   _____

UNIT 5

THE MANY FACES OF LOVE

UNIT 5

THE MANY FACES OF LOVE 97

A Rose for Emily

William Faulkner   *Moderate to Difficult*

SYNOPSIS

The story begins with the funeral of Miss Emily Grierson, the last of one of this Southern town's "old" families and a recluse who, for many years, has seen no one but her black servant. As a young girl, she had had suitors, all of whom were discouraged by her father. After his death, she was ill for a while. That was the year that a construction job brought a Yankee, Homer Barron, to town. He began "courting" Miss Emily, but boasted to other men that he was not the "marrying kind." When he "went away," the neighbors were not surprised; but after Emily's death, when they broke open the door to an upstairs room, they found Homer in the bed where he had lain dead for forty years!

SUGGESTION

To help students understand Miss Emily and her motivation for killing Homer Barron, it may be necessary to review and discuss clues Faulkner offers: her family's haughty attitude; hints of insanity in Emily's background; her father's discouraging her earlier suitors; her behavior upon her father's death; and the arrival of the cousins who probably made Emily face the fact that Homer was destroying her reputation.

ANSWER KEY

1. She pays no taxes; no one dared to approach her about the peculiar odor.
2. They are proud people, and respected because they are one of the "good families."
3. No one suspects; the druggist doesn't pursue his question about the poison.
4. Whether she loved or hated him, he was all she had.
5. big, dashing, full of fun
6. He was unlike anyone else she had known.
7. Answers will vary. She was determined to save face and get revenge.
8. Answers will vary. She was carrying out a wedding-night ritual.
9. It was the only way she could keep him; also, she realized he had taken advantage of her.

Reading Quiz:

Exploring the Labyrinths of the Mind

Name: _____

Date: _____

A Rose for Emily

Considering and answering the following questions should help you understand Miss Emily's motivations—her reasons for doing things. Each question requires only a one-sentence answer, but choose your words carefully.

1. What indications are there that no one in town would dare to check up on Miss Emily?

   _____

   _____

2. What does the answer to question #1 imply about Emily and her family?

   _____

   _____

3. How does the attitude of the townspeople toward her work in Emily's favor when she decides to commit a crime?

   _____

   _____

4. Why do you suppose Emily did not, at first, accept her father's death?

   _____

   _____

5. How is Homer Barron described in the story?

   _____

   _____

(continued)

A Rose for Emily (continued)

6. Why do you think he had special appeal for Emily?

_____

_____

7. What effect do you think the cousins' visit had on Emily?

_____

_____

8. Why do you suppose she bought the clothing and toilet articles for Homer Barron?

_____

_____

9. If Miss Emily loved Homer, why did she kill him?

_____

_____

See How They Run

Mary Elizabeth Vroman   *Easy*

SYNOPSIS

Jane Richards, a young, enthusiastic third-grade teacher, faces her class of 43 black children for the first time and realizes they are a cross-section of her people, from very poor to well-to-do. As the term progresses, she tries hard to help every child, but a few become especially important to her. One is beautiful little Tanya, who dies that year of diphtheria; another is C.T., poor, proud, generous, but apparently indifferent to school. Eventually, she "reaches" C.T. and shows him that lessons can be worthwhile. He is her greatest success, but as she watches the children leave on the last day, she knows she has helped all of them to grow in self-esteem.

SUGGESTION

The title of this short story is taken from the old round, "Three Blind Mice." The author makes the point that the "farmer's wife," whose long arm reaches out to cut off the mice's tails (stifle the children's talents and destroy them) is actually the combination of "circumstances, their environment, and heredity." Ask the students if they can show how the story illustrates that idea. The quiz emphasizes some of the incidents they'll want to look at, for example, the principal's attitude, other teachers' attitudes, and C.T.'s indifference to learning.

ANSWER KEY

1. E	7. J
2. F	8. D
3. B	9. I
4. C	10. H
5. G	11. C
6. A	12. C

Name: _____

Date: _____

See How They Run

Match the descriptions in Column A with the characters in Column B.

Column A

_____ 1. Her father is a Methodist minister; her family is relatively well-to-do; she is self-confident.

_____ 2. He is named for a famous black educator.

_____ 3. She is an eager young teacher.

_____ 4. He has little respect for learning and spends two years in each grade.

_____ 5. He is very bright and is named for a famous heavyweight champion.

_____ 6. Her method of handling students is to beat them into submission.

_____ 7. He is the harried principal who believes that if the school is quiet, the children are learning.

_____ 8. Poverty was the real cause of her death.

_____ 9. He is engaged to the third-grade teacher.

_____ 10. He is a kind man, but is prejudiced against blacks.

_____ 11. He stole a rose for his classmate's grave.

_____ 12. His "pop" said that too much studying would "eat out yer brains."

Column B

A. Miss Nelson

B. Jane Richards

C. C.T. Young

D. Tanya Fulton

E. Rachel Smith

F. Booker T. Adams

G. Joe Louis

H. Doctor Sinclair

I. Paul Carlyle

J. Mr. Johnson

150 Great Short Stories

The Duke's Children

Frank O'Connor   *Easy*

SYNOPSIS

Larry Delaney is a romantic. Although he is only a messenger boy, he is certain he is of noble birth, by some unkind quirk of fate set down among people who are not worthy of him. Actually, his father, who works in the manure factory, is a lively man, interested in world events and eager to talk. Larry is ashamed of him and embarrassed when Nancy Harding, the girl he wants to impress, meets his father. When Larry is not invited to the Harding house, he is certain that his family and his poverty are to blame. Much later, when he is dating the matter-of-fact May Dwyer, he meets Nancy again and discovers that she, like him, was ashamed of her background.

SUGGESTION

The title of this story is ironic. Students should see that what appears to be true is not. Far from being the duke's children, Larry and Nancy are ordinary young people, from ordinary families, who do not accept the realities of their environment.

ANSWER KEY

1. C		9. B	
2. C		10. D	
3. F		11. F	
4. A		12. F	
5. B		13. E	
6. C		14. C	
7. F		15. A	
8. C			

Name: _____

Date: _____

The Duke's Children

Match the descriptions in Column A with the characters in Column B.

Column A

_____ 1. Was certain he was of noble birth

_____ 2. Thought his own family, especially his father, didn't measure up

_____ 3. Waited eagerly each day for the newspaper

_____ 4. Had no pretense whatsoever about her

_____ 5. Really was fond of Larry and jealous of his new girl

_____ 6. Claimed to be able to speak several languages

_____ 7. Was an entertaining talker whose war experiences were his favorite topic

_____ 8. Was a messenger boy, but eventually got "sacked"

_____ 9. "Accidentally" met Larry several times

_____ 10. Was small, with a face like a clenched fist, and carried his newspaper like a baton

_____ 11. Worked in the manure factory

_____ 12. Liked Nancy but thought she was quite a talker

_____ 13. Argued with Larry about the state of the country, but they became fast friends

_____ 14. Told Nancy's father that he planned to take the Indian Civil Service exam

_____ 15. Asked Larry if he could afford the tram fare

Column B

A. May Dwyer

B. Nancy Harding

C. Larry Delaney

D. Mr. Harding

E. Mr. Dwyer

F. Mr. Delaney

A Summer Tragedy

Arna Bontemps   *Easy*

SYNOPSIS

Jeff Patton, a black sharecropper for more than 50 years, is dressing himself in his best clothes. But his hands tremble so that he cannot manage his bowtie, and he has to ask his blind wife, Jennie, for assistance. When both have put on their ancient "finery," they start out in their Model T. They talk little, but the reader learns what is on Jeff's mind: Since his stroke, he hasn't the strength to work the land, and his crop will not be enough to get them out of debt. He knows another stroke would leave him dependent on frail Jennie. Seeing no other choice, the two have agreed on this "journey," which ends when Jeff deliberately aims the old Ford down a slope and into the river.

SUGGESTION

"A Summer Tragedy" was published during the depression years of the early 1930's. In a class discussion, students might explore what other choices were available to the two old people and what other choices would be available to them today.

ANSWER KEY

1. 50 years
2. Baby
3. being a burden to Jenny
4. has never forgiven Old Delia for smiling at him years ago
5. the Mardi Gras
6. protective
7. slightly impatient
8. They don't want to be separated.
9. Answers will vary.

Reading Quiz:

An Unusual Love Story

Name: _____

Date: _____

A *Summer Tragedy*

    If you read the story carefully and understand the two characters, you'll find it easy to answer the following questions.

1. How long have Jeff and Jennie been married?

   _____

   _____

2. What term of endearment does he still use in speaking to her?

   _____

   _____

3. If he should have another stroke, what does he fear most?

   _____

   _____

4. How do we know Jennie still has a lingering jealousy where Jeff is concerned?

   _____

   _____

5. What is one of the last things Jeff remembers?

   _____

   _____

6. What adjective would you use to describe Jeff's attitude toward Jennie?

   _____

7. What adjective describes her attitude toward him?

   _____

8. Aside from financial problems, what other reason do you think they have for their suicide pact?

   _____

   _____

9. What effect did the story have on you? Explain briefly.

   _____

   _____

To Hell with Dying

Alice Walker   *Moderate*

SYNOPSIS

The narrator remembers Mr. Sweet, a black man, as "a diabetic and an alcoholic and a guitar player" who was a neighbor when she was growing up. Frequently, he claimed to be about to die, but her father would revive him by saying, "To hell with dying, Man, the children want Mr. Sweet." The children took part in these revivals by climbing onto his bed and kissing and tickling him until he began to laugh, for he was their friend and playmate even though he was ancient. The narrator is twenty-five and Mr. Sweet is over ninety when her parents call her home for the last revival. This time, Mr. Sweet opens his eyes, smiles at her, and dies.

SUGGESTION

In this tender and humorous short story, Alice Walker portrays a very special relationship between young children and an old man. Ask the students to describe orally or in essay-form an elderly person—relative or friend—who is or was important in their lives.

ANSWER KEY

1. He realized he wouldn't be accepted "above" his station.

2. His good humor doesn't fail him even though he knows the boy is weak.

3. It makes Mr. Sweet think he amounts to something after all.

4. It is a measure of Mr. Sweet's love that he wanted her to have what he valued most.

To Hell with Dying

Although this is a story about aging and death, it is also a story about life, told with humor and understanding. Mr. Sweet is portrayed as a man who did not realize his dream, but who retained his sense of humor and gave much love. Keeping that in mind, you are to state briefly what you think is the significance of each of the following quotations from the story.

1. "Mr. Sweet had been ambitious as a boy, wanted to be a doctor or a lawyer or a sailor, only to find that black man fare better if they are not."

   _____

   _____

2. Mr. Sweet's son "was shiftless as the day is long and spent money as if he were trying to see the bottom of the mint, which Mr. Sweet would tell him was the clean brown palm of his hand."

   _____

   _____

3. The narrator explains that her brother would sometimes play Mr. Sweet's guitar, "in fact, pretend that he was a young version of Mr. Sweet, and it always made Mr. Sweet glad that someone wanted to be like him."

   _____

   _____

4. Before he died, Mr. Sweet asked the narrator's parents to give her the guitar, because "he had known that even if I came next time, he would not be able to respond in the old way. He did not want me to feel that my trip had been for nothing."

   _____

   _____

A Day in the Country

Anton Chekhov

Easy

SYNOPSIS

Fyokla, a six-year-old beggar girl, runs through the village looking for her friend, Terenty the cobbler. She needs help. Her eight-year-old brother Danilka has caught his hand in a hole in a tree, trying to get a cuckoo's egg for her. Terenty must come. He does; then the old man and the boy wander the rest of the day through fields and woods, talking of birds, flowers, everything in nature. The little girl trails behind. At night, the children go to a deserted barn to sleep, and Terenty goes to the tavern. Later he comes back, blesses the sleeping children, and leaves bread for them.

SUGGESTION

If the students have not read any other Chekhov stories, you might point out that this one is typical: its mood of gentle melancholy; the peasants whose life, by our standards, is grim; their acceptance of their lot; the poor little beggar children; the scarecrowlike old man; and the story's ending, resolving nothing.

ANSWER KEY

1. six and eight
2. begging, sleeping in deserted places
3. cobbler
4. nature
5. trying to get a cuckoo egg for his sister
6. prays after eating, prays over the children
7. "Why should it kill a little thing like you?"
8. forest; the count
9. freight train
10. nature itself

Name: _____

Date: _____

A Day in the Country

Chances are that this short story is unlike most of the others you have read. It mirrors another time and place: Russia in the nineteenth century. If you can answer the following questions, you've learned a bit about Russia and about the characters in the story. Be brief.

1. _____ How old are Fyokla and Danilka?

2. _____ How do they get food and shelter?

3. _____ What is Terenty's trade?

4. _____ As they walk and talk, what is Terenty teaching Danilka about?

5. _____ How did Danilka get his hand caught?

6. _____ What indications are there that Terenty is a religious man?

7. _____ How does Terenty try to comfort Fyokla when she hears the thunder?

8. _____ Fyokla tells Terenty that Danilka is in the *copse*. What do you think that word means? Who owns the copse?

9. _____ The three friends see a goods train, and Terenty tries to explain the working of the steam engine. What do we call a goods train?

10. _____ Chekhov tells us that not only Terenty, but also the innkeeper, the market gardener, the shepherd—in fact, all the villagers—are knowledgeable about nature. Who was their teacher?

How the Mountains Are

Jesse Hill Ford   *Easy*

SYNOPSIS

Mary takes care of a cranky invalid. Her brother Albert, a chauffeur, tells her of a summer job taking care of his employer's two little boys. Eager to see the mountains and certain that the children would be a pleasanter responsibility than the invalid, Mary goes. She loves her two small charges and watches them closely, for the summer home is built on a cliffside. One day the boys' mother asks Mary to bring the the children down to meet visitors, promising to watch them while Mary takes her bath. But the mother becomes engrossed in her bridge game, and if not for Mary, the boys might have fallen and been killed.

SUGGESTION

The students should be aware of the irony in this story: On Mary's first day, Mrs. St. John chides her for not watching the children closely enough, yet the one time Mary is not with them the children come close to a tragic accident because their mother is so engrossed in her bridge game.

ANSWER KEY

1. H	6. E or F	11. G
2. I	7. E or F	12. I
3. G	8. B	13. H
4. C	9. H	14. H
5. D	10. B	15. A

Name: _____

Date: _____

How the Mountains Are

In this exercise, you are asked to match the descriptions in Column A with the characters in Column B.

Column A

_____ 1. A forty-year-old nurse

_____ 2. A chauffeur

_____ 3. A well-to-do woman, mother of two small boys

_____ 4. A chubby, affectionate three-year-old

_____ 5. His five-year-old brother

_____ 6. A black poodle with a curly mane

_____ 7. Another black poodle

_____ 8. A mountain "native"

_____ 9. The person who saved the children from falling

_____ 10. The person who offered to take the children fishing

_____ 11. The person who was too interested in the bridge game to watch the children

_____ 12. He found the job for his sister.

_____ 13. She thought the mountains were very beautiful.

_____ 14. The children wondered if she was once a slave.

_____ 15. Someone tipped over his chair at the card table.

Column B

A. Mr. Brassfield

B. Beelah

C. Little Phil

D. Went

E. Fritz

F. Mr. Marmaduke

G. Mrs. St. John

H. Mary

I. Albert

150 Great Short Stories

Barrow Street

Richard Sherman   Moderate

SYNOPSIS

In an attractively furnished apartment of a New York brownstone, a young woman moves restlessly from room to room. Finally, the phone call she is expecting comes—a former boyfriend in town for the night has wired her to expect him. But now, since she has told him she is married, he hesitates to come to see her. She persuades him. At first he is surprised that three years have changed her so much. She is married, has a child, is more confident, and is obviously prosperous. After a few drinks he tries to make love to her, but she dismisses him. Shortly, the owners of the apartment return, pay her for babysitting, and the masquerade is over.

SUGGESTION

"Barrow Street" has a surprise ending, but the author gave a number of clues that should have alerted careful readers that something was not as it seemed. Ask students if any details puzzled them. For example, why was the young woman wearing a "serviceable" black dress if she owned a closet full of expensive ones and was expecting a visitor?

ANSWER KEY

1. George walked out.

2. hated George, wished he was dead, wished she was dead herself

3. wants a permanent relationship

4. Dorothy; George didn't want to get involved.

5. Yes; she almost responds to him, but is determined to have revenge.

6. No; she checks the bottle to see how much is left.

7. revenge; also, doesn't trust herself

Name: _____

Date: _____

Barrow Street

If you read the story carefully, you know quite a bit about George and Dorothy's relationship, present and past. Answering the following questions will pinpoint the details.

1. What or who broke off the relationship three years ago?

   _____

   _____

2. In Dorothy's own words, how did she feel after their break-up?

   _____

   _____

3. In George's words, what is wrong with his new love affair?

   _____

   _____

4. In their earlier relationship, which one wanted it to be permanent?

   _____

   _____

5. Does Dorothy still love George? Explain.

   _____

   _____

6. Has Dorothy conquered her drinking habit? How do you know?

   _____

   _____

7. Why did Dorothy go to so much trouble to make George think she was happily married?

   _____

   _____

Our Lady's Juggler

Anatole France   *Easy*

SYNOPSIS

Long ago in France lived a juggler called Barnaby. Skilled in his art
though he was, he barely earned a living, for he could only perform in
summer at fairs. He lived simply and cheerfully, being very devoted to the
Blessed Virgin. One evening he chanced to meet a monk. They talked, and
the monk, recognizing Barnaby's faith, invited him to join the monastery
where he was the prior. Once there, Barnaby discovered that each of the
monks, all learned men, paid special tribute to the Virgin, according to their
talents. But Barnaby thought sadly that he had no special talent. Then he had
an inspiration—each day after that, the juggler, in the deserted chapel, performed for Our Lady.

SUGGESTION

Anatole France's lovely little story of a minor miracle is a retelling of a
legend that dates back to the Middle Ages. In this version, the prior states
the theme, "Blessed are the simple-hearted, for they shall see God." You
might help the students to see another theme too—that it makes no difference what kind of work one does; if it is done with a loving heart, it is
acceptable to God.

ANSWER KEY

1. France, in the time of Louis
2. juggling
3. can work only in summer
4. the Virgin Mary
5. recognizes his goodness
6. He has no special skill to honor the Virgin.
7. is inspired to juggle for her
8. because Barnaby goes often to the empty chapel
9. monks disapprove; prior thinks he is mad
10. They witness a miracle.

Reading Quiz:
Thinking It Over

Name: _____

Date: _____

Our Lady's Juggler

Each of the following questions requires only a brief answer; in some cases one word is enough.

1. _____ When and where is the story set?

2. _____ What is Barnaby's means of making a living?

3. _____ Since he is skillful at what he does, why does he have trouble earning enough for food and shelter?

4. _____ To whom is Barnaby completely devoted?

5. _____ Why does the prior invite him to live at the monastery?

6. _____ After entering the monastery, why is Barnaby sad?

7. _____ How does he solve his problem?

8. _____ Why does the prior become curious or suspicious about Barnaby?

9. _____ When the monks and the prior first see what Barnaby is doing, what is their reaction?

10. _____ What changes their minds?

The Old Bird, a Love Story

J.F. Powers   Moderate

SYNOPSIS

Unemployed and elderly, Mr. Newman is one of several people filling out job applications and waiting to be interviewed. He is painfully eager, and shows it. The personnel man does hire him and puts him to work in the shipping room. This is a comedown for Mr. Newman, who is used to "white-collar" jobs. All day he tries desperately to show his efficiency, but is deflated when he overhears a conversation between his supervisor and the personnel director: "If this keeps up, we'll have to draft them from the old people's home." But back home that night, he resumes his usual role of "man of the world" for his loving audience of one, his wife.

SUGGESTION

Powers' story has both humor and pathos. Mr. Newman's initial struggle with twine and paper and his vain attempt to fool his audience of one are funny, and the students will probably see them that way. But they should also see that his "jauntiness" and his pride in the company where he is only a "temporary" are pitiful attempts to convince himself and the world that he is not just a "has-been," an "old bird."

ANSWER KEY

1. B		6. H	
2. A		7. I	
3. C		8. E	
4. D		9. G	
5. F		10. J	

Reading Quiz:

Noticing the Details Which Reveal Character

The Old Bird, A Love Story

In Column A are incomplete statements about the characters' actions; in Column B are the reasons for those actions. Your job is to match the two.

Column A

_____ 1. Mr. Newman cherishes his orange fountain pen with the green ink because he _____ .

_____ 2. He is afraid of making any mistake in his application because he _____ .

_____ 3. Mrs. Newman remains her husband's faithful audience of one, seeming to believe his fibs, because she _____ .

_____ 4. Mr. Hurley is brusque when he tells Mr. Newman the details of the job, and doesn't bother to give him the location of the employees' lunchroom because he _____ .

_____ 5. Hurley's remarks to the personnel director about Mr. Newman show that he _____ .

_____ 6. When Mr. Newman says, "Got an application there for a retired millionaire?" to the receptionist, he is _____ .

_____ 7. She laughs at that and smiles at him because she _____ .

_____ 8. When Hurley suggests that Mr. Newman stop work a little early, he is _____ .

_____ 9. Shanahan, the personnel man, hires Mr. Newman because he _____ .

_____ 10. Mr. Newman buys a newspaper to read on the streetcar and tells the seller to keep the change because he _____ .

Column B

A. wants the job desperately

B. wants to preserve some individuality

C. has the tolerance that is part of love

D. is a self-important man

E. attempting clumsily to be kind

F. is prejudiced about age

G. recognizes that Newman will not argue about salary

H. trying to appear jaunty, but fears rejection

I. has some sympathy for him

J. wants to think that he is still a prosperous businessman

UNIT 6

TALES WITH A TWIST ====

Get Ready for Some Surprise Endings

UNIT 6

TALES WITH A TWIST
Get Ready for Some Surprise Endings **121**

The Gift of the Magi

O. Henry   *Easy*

<u>SYNOPSIS</u>

Della is miserable on Christmas Eve because she has been able to save only $1.87 from her grocery money to buy a gift for her husband, Jim. Then she thinks of another source for cash, selling her beautiful brown hair, and she does, for $20.00. Supplemented by the grocery money, it is enough to buy a platinum chain for Jim's most valued possession, his father's gold watch. Della is not prepared for Jim's reaction when he sees her shorn head—astonishment and disbelief—for he has sold his watch to buy combs for her long hair. But O. Henry points out that each has given the other the greatest of gifts, unselfish love.

<u>SUGGESTION</u>

Because "The Gift of the Magi" is such a touching story, it remains popular despite its nineteenth-century style. Ask the students to point out old-fashioned word choices and examples of the author's speaking directly to the reader as no modern writer would.

ANSWER KEY

1. bulldozing
2. Christmas Eve
3. Jim makes only $20 a week.
4. Della's hair and Jim's watch
5. $20; her hair
6. a platinum chain
7. combs for her hair
8. pretty
9. disbelief
10. love

Name: _____

Date: _____

The Gift of the Magi

Complete each of the following sentences in the fewest possible words.

1. _____ Della had saved $1.87 by the unpleasant means of _____ the grocer and the vegetable man and the butcher.

2. _____ When the story opens, the time is _____ .

3. _____ The name on the mail box, James Dillingham Young, now seems a little pretentious because _____ .

4. _____ The James Dillingham Youngs' most precious possessions are _____ and _____ .

5. _____ Madame Safronie gives Della _____ for _____ .

6. _____ Della's Christmas present to Jim was _____ .

7. _____ His gift to her was _____ .

8. _____ Della was afraid that Jim would think she was no longer _____ .

9. _____ Jim's reaction when he came home was _____ .

10. _____ The most important gift that Jim and Della gave each other was _____ .

A Mother in Mannville

Marjorie Kinnan Rawlings   *Easy*

SYNOPSIS

The narrator, a writer, hires a cabin on the property of an orphanage in the Carolina mountains and tells the administrator she needs one of the boys to chop wood for her fireplace. She thinks the undersized twelve-year-old who comes will not be able to do the job. But Jerry is so responsible and hardworking that she soon comes to depend on him, and their friendship grows. He tells her that he is luckier than most, for his mother lives in Mannville and often sends him gifts. Secretly, she wonders how any woman could abandon a boy like Jerry. When she is leaving, she learns that Jerry's mother is only the lonely boy's dream.

SUGGESTION

Rawlings's characterization of Jerry is very effective, yet the reader is never told what the boy is thinking and is left to judge him by his actions and by the narrator's comments about him. Ask the students to compile a list of adjectives which describe Jerry and to be ready to defend each choice.

ANSWER KEY

1. B	9. A
2. A	10. C
3. B	11. B
4. B	12. B
5. A	13. B or C
6. A	14. A
7. B	15. C
8. B	

Reading Quiz:

Describing the Characters

Name: _____

Date: _____

A Mother in Mannville

This short story has only two characters, so your first task is an easy one—to decide whether each of the adjectives listed below describes A, the narrator; B, Jerry; or C, either one.

1. _____ Undersized

2. _____ Reluctant to form ties to put down roots

3. _____ Highly dependable

4. _____ Industrious

5. _____ Basically kindhearted

6. _____ Sometimes matter-of-fact or blunt

7. _____ Sensitive and tactful

8. _____ Good with animals

9. _____ Widely traveled

10. _____ Appreciative of nature

11. _____ Proud

12. _____ Naturally courteous

13. _____ Lonely

14. _____ Sometimes engrossed in work

15. _____ Reluctant to face saying good-bye

16. Finally, the narrator describes Jerry as having "integrity." What does that word signify to you?

_____

_____

_____

The Open Window

Saki

Easy

<u>SYNOPSIS</u>

Frampton Nuttel, a nervous young man, is waiting to pay a courtesy call on Mrs. Sappleton. He has a letter of introduction from his sister, who was determined that he would not be lonely during his country rest-cure. Until Mrs. Sappleton comes downstairs, her niece, Vera, a self-possessed fifteen-year-old, is "entertaining" the visitor. Having made certain that Nuttel is unacquainted in the neighborhood, she tells him of her aunt's great tragedy: Three years before, her husband and two young brothers had gone through the now open French doors, off on a hunting trip from which they never returned. When Mrs. Sappleton finally appears, she is cheerful enough, but the reappearance of her husband and brothers completely unnerves Nuttel, who takes an abrupt leave.

<u>SUGGESTION</u>

Saki's closing sentence—"Romance at short notice was her specialty"—explains Vera's elaborate fabrications, but its significance will be lost on the students if they equate romance with boy-meets-girl. A dictionary or, preferably, a literary dictionary will acquaint them with the meaning of *romance* that Saki intended.

ANSWER KEY

1. A		6. A	
2. B		7. A	
3. D		8. A	
4. E, C		9. B	
5. C		10. A	

127

The Open Window

Match the descriptions in Column A with the characters in Column B.

Column A

_____ 1. Was in the country for his nerves

_____ 2. Had a lively imagination

_____ 3. Was well meaning and polite, but a bit vague

_____ 4. Had been off hunting

_____ 5. Was fond of "Bertie, why do you bound?"

_____ 6. Had a sister who apparently mothered him

_____ 7. Was easily "taken in"

_____ 8. Thought he had seen ghosts

_____ 9. Was actually cruel and got "kicks" from others' discomfort

_____ 10. Talked at length about his illness

Column B

A. Frampton Nuttel

B. Vera

C. Ronnie

D. Mrs. Sappleton

E. Mr. Sappleton

Desirée's Baby

Kate Chopin

Moderate

SYNOPSIS

Long before the story opens, a toddler was discovered at the gates of the Valmondé plantation. She was brought up with much love by the childless Valmondés and eventually fell in love with the proud scion of the Aubigny family who owned the neighboring plantation. The two young people, Armand and Desirée, were married despite Monsieur Valmondé's warning to Armand that nothing was known of Desirée's real family. But when Desirée bore a child that was unmistakably a quadroon, her husband denounced her, and she went away, heartbroken. Only then did he come upon an old letter and learn that it was his own mother who was "of the race that is cursed with the brand of slavery."

SUGGESTION

Kate Chopin, whose own mother was a Creole, wrote excellent local-color stories of these Louisiana people in whose lives tradition was and is very important. Students need to know that this story was first published in 1894 and is set in an earlier time; it will help them understand the pride and prejudice the story portrays.

ANSWER KEY

1. been found at their gate

2. had been born in and lived in Paris until then

3. mistress

4. Paris

5. Nothing was known of Desirée's origin.

6. a quadroon

7. white

8. go

9. drowns herself and her child

10. black

Reading Quiz:

Fitting the Pieces of the Puzzle Together

Name: _____

Date: _____

Desirée's Baby

In a story with a surprise ending, the author must set the scene in such a way that even though the conclusion is not what the reader expected, he or she realizes it could have happened that way. In this exercise, filling in the blanks will help you to review the sequence of events.

_____ 1. Desirée was not the natural child of the Valmondés; instead, she had _____ .

_____ 2. Armand did not see Desirée until he was eight years old because he _____ .

_____ 3. L'Abrie, the Aubigny plantation, had a desolate look because for many years it had no _____ .

_____ 4. Armand's mother had lived and died in _____ .

_____ 5. When Armand and Desirée were about to be married, M. Valmondé warned him that _____ .

_____ 6. Before Desirée does, her mother, the blacks, and the neighbors, as well as her husband, all realize that her baby is _____ .

_____ 7. When she confronts her husband, he tells her that she is not _____ .

_____ 8. When she tells him that her mother has asked her to come home, he tells her to _____ .

_____ 9. After she leaves the plantation, she actually _____ .

_____ 10. Only when Armand finds the scrap of an old letter from his mother to his father does he know that it was his mother who was _____ .

The Ambitious Guest

Nathaniel Hawthorne

Moderate

SYNOPSIS

On a wild September night, a family sits around the fire in their mountain home—father, mother, children, and grandmother. Because their house is on a road that runs through a notch of the White Mountains of New Hampshire, travelers occasionally stop for a night's lodging. Tonight, a young man knocks on their door and is accepted at their fireside. In a kind of strange intimacy (inspired perhaps by the storm and their isolation), each person, from the youngest to the oldest, reveals an ambition. The stranger's is to acquire lasting fame. But that is not to be; a rock slide buries them all as they attempt to flee. Only the house remains.

SUGGESTION

Hawthorne based "The Ambitious Guest" on an actual historical incident, the rock slide in Crawford Notch which left no survivors of the Willey family. This short story is a good one to illustrate the way the writer of fiction may "embroider" history to suit his purpose. Obviously, we have no way of knowing what the family talked about that night, or whether or not a stranger was with them.

ANSWER KEY

1. the father

2. the little boy

3. the grandmother

4. the ambitious guest

5. the eldest daughter

6. It is not known whether or not he existed.

Reading Quiz:

A Story of Dreams and Aspirations

Name: _____

Date: _____

The Ambitious Guest

The imaginary conversation of the family and their guest seated around the fire fascinates readers who know the actual fate of these people. If you can identify each person by his or her wish or dream, you have read the story carefully.

1. _____ "I was wishing we had a good farm in Bartlett, or Bethelehem, or Littleton . . . I should want to stand well with my neighbors . . . and go to general court for a term or two."

2. _____ "I want . . . all of us, and the stranger too . . . to go and take a drink out of the basin of the Flume."

3. _____ "I want one of you . . . when your mother is dressed and in the coffin . . . to hold a looking-glass over my face."

4. _____ "I cannot die until I have achieved my destiny. Then let death come! I shall have built my monument."

5. _____ "It is better to sit here by the fire and be comfortable and contented, though nobody thinks about us."

6. In the conclusion of the story, what does the author tell you about the ambitious guest?

_____

_____

_____

Gal Young Un

Marjorie Kinnan Rawlings   *Moderate*

SYNOPSIS

A middle-aged widow, Mattie Syles, lives in isolation in the Florida woods. She is so hungry for company that when two hunters chance by, she offers to cook them a meal. They decline, but not long after, the younger, Trax Colton, comes upon her house again and lingers to eat her food and impress her with what he has seen and done. An opportunist, when he hears that she has money he marries her and uses her money to set up a still. Soon he buys an expensive car and expands his territory, leaving Mattie to run the still. Then Trax comes home briefly, bringing the girl Ellie with him. Eventually, Mattie gets her revenge, and Trax goes off, defeated, leaving her and the Gal Young Un to themselves.

SUGGESTION

In "Gal Young Un" Marjorie Kinnan Rawlings gives a detailed picture of Florida in the 1920's and '30's, one that is probably unfamiliar to the students. Turpentine wagons, stills, moonshine, bootlegging, even a house built of unpainted cypress and the term *hammock* may puzzle young readers. Finding the meaning or significance of each would make a worthwhile library assignment.

ANSWER KEY

1. F	6. A	11. E
2. E	7. B	12. A
3. C	8. A	13. A
4. D	9. A	14. E
5. B	10. E	15. A

Gal Young Un

In Column A are descriptions of the characters in Column B. Match descriptions and characters.

Column A

_____ 1. Tried to warn Mattie about Trax

_____ 2. Was still cutting out paper dolls

_____ 3. Was a hunter with some manners; gave Mattie a quail

_____ 4. Worked at the still

_____ 5. Took advantage of everyone

_____ 6. Knew she was plain

_____ 7. Had a way with women

_____ 8. Burned up Trax's car and broke up the still

_____ 9. Was lonely and eager to talk to passersby

_____ 10. Had a "Pa" who deserted her when he went off with a woman

_____ 11. Loved Mattie's cat

_____ 12. Angrily skimped on the food she served

_____ 13. Had a kind heart and pitied the Gal Young Un

_____ 14. Was the Gal Young Un

_____ 15. At first, was happy to have Trax in her house

Column B

A. Mattie Syles

B. Trax Colton

C. Old Man Blaine

D. Lantry Brothers

E. Ellie

F. the storekeeper

Occurrence at Owl Creek Bridge

Ambrose Bierce   *Moderate*

SYNOPSIS

It is Civil War time. Federal soldiers are about to hang a man from Owl Creek Bridge. The man, Peyton Farquhar, a Southern planter, is thinking of his wife and children and is aware of the unbearably loud ticking of his watch as the sergeant steps aside to let the plank tilt. The rest of the story seems to be about Farquhar's miraculous escape and his all-day journey through a strange wood to reach at last his home and his loving wife. Then, in the final sentence, the reader is reminded that Farquhar is dead of a broken neck, and his body swings beneath Owl Creek Bridge.

SUGGESTION

This story fascinates students, but the for the careful readers among them, the closing sentence is not usually a surprise. Ask each student to describe what in the story, if anything, gave him or her a clue that Farquhar was dead even though he seemed to be making a remarkable escape.

ANSWER KEY

1. 1861–65

2. an attempt to destroy the bridge

3. slave-owning Southern gentleman

4. No.

5. The rope broke.

6. vortex or whirlpool

7. The river had been described repeatedly as *sluggish*.

8. It was wilder than he expected so close to home.

9. when the plank is tilted; in the dream, he was about to embrace his wife

10. Answers will vary.

Name: _____

Date: _____

Occurrence at Owl Creek Bridge

1. Within five years, date the incident in the story.

   _____

2. What was Farquhar's crime that brought about his punishment?

   _____

   _____

3. What was Farquhar's background?

   _____

   _____

4. Does the author explain why Farquhar was not in the army?

   _____

   _____

5. What reasonable explanation is given for Farquhar's apparently not being hanged when the plank tilted?

   _____

   _____

6. What natural phenomenon was responsible for Farquhar's reaching safety on the river bank?

   _____

   _____

7. In actuality, why was it unlikely that such a natural phenomenon would occur? (This calls for a deduction on your part.)

   _____

   _____

8. What puzzled Farquhar about the forest through which he traveled?

   _____

   _____

9. When did Farquhar actually die?

   _____

   _____

10. Did the ending surprise you? Explain briefly.

   _____

Dip in the Pool

Roald Dahl

Easy

SYNOPSIS

After some rough weather, the calm sea is relaxing the passengers, but a sudden storm soon sets the ship rolling again. Mr. Botibol, having made discreet inquiries of the purser, knows that the captain has already made his estimate of the ship's 24-hour mileage. Botibol decides that the new storm will slow the ship enough so that the "low field" in the evening's auction might win the pool. He buys that ticket, cleaning out his checking account to do it. Next morning, to his dismay, the sea is once more calm. He must slow the ship! To do that, he jumps overboard, making certain he has a witness. What Botibol doesn't know is that the witness is quite mad!

SUGGESTION

Ask the students what their reaction was to the ending of this story. Generally, they find Botibol an unsympathetic character, motivated by greed, and feel no particular regret that his scheme didn't work. It is worth pointing out that he is a pathetic character too, hoping to do something to give himself more status in his wife's eyes.

ANSWER KEY

1. high
2. storm
3. slackened speed
4. 200 pounds
5. savings

6. Lincoln convertible
7. is calm
8. jumping overboard
9. a witness
10. insane

Dip in the Pool

Complete the following statements in the fewest possible words.

_____ 1. Botibol is interested to know when the captain made his estimate "on the day's run" because he thinks the sudden storm may make that figure too _____ .

_____ 2. Mr. Botibol goes to the sun deck to make his own estimate of the _____ .

_____ 3. Mr. Botibol asks the elevator man if he thinks the ship has _____ .

_____ 4. Mr. Botibol buys the ticket on the low field for (amount) _____ .

_____ 5. For him, that amounts to two years' _____ .

_____ 6. With his winnings, he dreams of buying his wife a _____ .

_____ 7. When Botibol wakes up in the morning, he is terribly upset because the sea _____ .

_____ 8. His plan to slow the ship involves _____ .

_____ 9. Before jumping, he makes certain he has _____ .

_____ 10. Unfortunately, he does not realize that his witness is _____ .

The Sniper

Liam O'Flaherty   *Easy*

SYNOPSIS

The scene is Dublin during the Civil War of the 1920's, which pitted Free Staters against Republicans (those who accepted the new treaty against those who wanted all Ireland free from British rule). A Republican sniper, concealed on a rooftop, lights a cigarette and draws enemy fire. Unharmed, he crawls to another position. When an armored car advances up the street, an old woman informs on him to the turret gunner, but the sniper kills both the gunner and the woman. Again, he is fired upon from a neighboring rooftop. Although he is wounded, he uses a ruse to draw his enemy out. He shoots the enemy and watches the body fall to the street below. Later, he discovers the dead man was his brother.

SUGGESTION

A provocative question to ask students who read this story is why O'Flaherty gave the sniper no name. Perceptive students will realize that he repesents any soldier made brutal by war. Also, since this was a civil war, it made relatives and friends into enemies.

ANSWER KEY

1. Dublin

2. a student

3. an old woman

4. sniper kills both gunner and woman

5. places his cap over the muzzle of the rifle and raises it; man on the opposite roof shoots at the cap

6. joy

7. remorse

8. The revolver he threw down goes off, and a bullet whizzes past his ear.

9. discovers the dead man was his brother

10. It is futile and makes men brutal fanatics.

Name: _____

Date: _____

The Sniper

Answer the following questions in as few words as possible.

1. _____ Where does the story take place?

2. _____ In peace time, what was the sniper's likely occupation?

3. _____ Who tells the turret gunner that the sniper is on the roof?

4. _____ What happens then?

5. _____ How does the wounded sniper trick the enemy?

6. _____ What is the sniper's first reaction after shooting his enemy?

7. _____ When the enemy's body falls to the pavement below, what is the sniper's reaction?

8. _____ What brings the sniper back to his senses?

9. _____ What final shock does the sniper face that day?

10. _____ What does the author seem to be saying about war?

Panic

Donn Byrne   *Easy*

SYNOPSIS

Guiseppe Pagino, a naive young Italian shopkeeper, comes to New York to make his fortune and is put in charge of a mob-owned grocery store in Little Italy. Each week, a "collector" comes to clean out the till, leaving Guiseppe only $12 for himself. One day, a notorious gunman, Squint Lacy, comes in and demands $10. Guiseppe's neighbor-shopkeeper, a more worldly Italian, tells Guiseppe that this is only the beginning of the "shake-down." After Lacy comes back for a second $10, the neighbor volunteers to confront the gunman next time. Lacy, who is "on the run," stops into the shop only long enough to repay his debt to Pagino, whom he calls "a square little guy." The "helpful" neighbor pockets the $20 and tells Guiseppe that he has vanquished the enemy.

SUGGESTION

Ask the students to look for and list references in the story that date it. For example: the lithograph of Victor Emmanuel (a student could be assigned to find out who he was); the delivery wagons, trolley cars, and horse-drawn fire engine; and, of course, Guiseppe's pay of $12 a week. Then, in class, students could compare lists and decide what changes would be needed to modernize the story. Finally, they should decide whether or not the incidents could take place today.

ANSWER KEY

1. green like Tokay
2. blue like shallow water
3. the desire that sent Caesar into Gaul and Caligula among the Teutons
4. making much money, just like Carnegie, just like Rothschild
5. gliding like gondolas
6. like some infernal chariot on which Pluto might have ridden
7. wolves
8. a cynical bulldog
9. a Chinese pagoda
10. a tiger; a rabbit
11. a Colossus
12. with the ease and grace of a cat
13. with the rapidity of a stage magician
14. with the air of a leading man making his departure from the stage

Name: _____

Date: _____

Panic

"Panic" contains many figures of speech—metaphors, similes, and allusions. As you know, metaphors (Squint Lacy's "bullet head" and "cauliflower" ear) and similes ("figs on a string like a rosary") are both comparisons. Allusions also make comparisons; for example, when Guiseppe's friend Michele, the coal and wood man, talks to the crowd about the great accomplishments of ancient Italians, the author says he speaks "as Cicero might have." Do you see that the allusion to Cicero, a great Roman statesman and orator, is also a comparison and, incidentally, a simile? See if you can find the metaphor, simile, or allusion which describes each of the following.

1. The olive oil on the grocery-store shelf:

   _____

2. Guiseppe's eyes:

   _____

3. Guiseppe's yearly springtime yearning to go wandering:

   _____

4. Guiseppe's words to his mother to describe his financial success in America:

   _____

5. The movement of the trolley cars:

   _____

6. The fire engine in motion:

   _____

7. In Guiseppe's mind, the animals to which the mobsters could be compared:

   _____

8. The animal that Squint Lacy's gap-toothed grin suggested?

   _____

(continued)

Panic (continued)

9. The building to which the coffee mill on the counter is compared:

   _____

10. In Guiseppe's dream confrontation with Squint, to what animal does he compare Squint?

    _____

    To what animal does he compare himself?

    _____

11. When Guiseppe looks out and sees the blue-coated vision, to what wonder of the ancient world does he compare the policeman?

    _____

12. The description of how Squint Lacy moves as he comes into Guiseppe's store for the last time:

    _____

13. The description of how Squint departed from the store:

    _____

14. The description of Michele's departure from Guiseppe's store:

    _____

UNIT 7

THE WAY WE WERE

Stories That Are Glimpses of the Past

UNIT 7

THE WAY WE WERE

Stories That Are Glimpses of the Past **145**

The Return of a Private

Hamlin Garland   *Moderate*

SYNOPSIS

The Civil War is over, and four soldiers are returning by train to their home state, Wisconsin, but their return is quite different from their send-off. Now no one seems interested in them. Three of them spend the night in the railroad station to save money before setting out at daylight for home. Smith, the main character, is so weak from fever that his buddy carries Smith's gun for him. Finally, they separate, and Smith goes on alone. His wife and three children have gone to their nearest neighbor's house this Sunday for companionship. They see Smith—scarcely recognizable—plodding past the gate and go hurrying after him. The reunion takes place in their own dooryard.

SUGGESTION

Point out to the students that Garland uses this rather somber story to show the futility and waste of war: the disruption of the life of ordinary men like this private; the indifference of society now that the former "heroes" are returning; the horror as exemplified in the death of Billie Tripp, who fell "with only a breath between a laugh and a death groan." Ask them to describe briefly any other short stories or novels they have read about war.

ANSWER KEY

1. Civil War
2. Wisconsin
3. Louisiana
4. to save money
5. fever, probably malaria
6. death of his buddy, Billie
7. homecoming, Sunday dinner
8. poorly; rented land to a neighbor who did not treat her fairly
9. No.
10. because she is lonely
11. from Mrs. Gray's reading of the tea leaves
12. He looks bent and sick.
13. The boy doesn't recognize him.
14. his old dog
15. biscuits and butter

Name: _____

Date: _____

The Return of a Private

Answer each question in the fewest possible words.

1. _____ From what war are the soldiers returning?

2. _____ What state is "home"?

3. _____ In what state did they fight?

4. _____ Why do three of them spend the night in the railroad station?

5. _____ What is Smith's physical ailment?

6. _____ What is his worst memory of the war?

7. _____ What do they dream of and talk about as they are walking?

8. _____ How has Smith's wife been getting along in his absence?

9. _____ Does she expect her husband?

10. _____ Why does she go with her children to Mother Gray's?

11. _____ What is the first inkling she gets that her husband is returning?

12. _____ Why isn't she certain that the soldier passing the Gray farm is her husband?

13. _____ What is sad about Smith's reunion with his youngest child?

14. _____ What does Smith miss in his homecoming?

15. _____ For what does Smith praise his wife to show how much he appreciates her?

Lucretia Burns

Hamlin Garland

Moderate

SYNOPSIS

Lucretia Burns, plain even as a girl, is now tired and faded from hard work, childbearing, and poverty. Married to Sim Burns, an Iowa farmer who never seems to get ahead and who now sees her more as a servant than anything else, Lucretia is overcome with hopelessness. For a few days she isolates herself as much as she can from her husband and her drudgery. Her sister-in-law attempts awkwardly to shake her out of her lethargy, but it is the pretty young schoolteacher, the antithesis of everything Lucretia has become, who finally persuades her to try again.

SUGGESTION

Students should know that in this short story, as in others he wrote, Garland presents a realistic picture of the life of prairie farmers, particularly emphasizing how difficult and unrewarding it could be for the women. The radical young Radbourn speaks for Garland himself when he offers what he believes are solutions to the farmers' plight.

ANSWER KEY

1. makes her think sadly of her girlhood
2. angry, unloving, indifferent
3. despairing
4. Answers will vary.
5. She is going crazy.
6. Lily: young, beautiful, hopeful, educated; Lucretia: middle-aged, plain, uneducated, hopeless
7. discontent
8. gives her sympathy, tells her Sim is sorry, points out that his life is as bleak as her own

Lucretia Burns

Answer each question briefly.

1. What effect does the beautiful spring evening have on Lucretia?

   _____

   _____

2. Describe briefly what kind of relationship Sim and Lucretia Burns now have.

   _____

   _____

3. Use one adjective to describe Lucretia's mood as she milks the last cow.

   _____

4. Garland says of Sim Burns and the way he lived and worked: "His life was mainly regulated from without." What does that statement mean to you?

   _____

   _____

5. When Lucretia's sister-in-law tries in vain to talk to her and find out what is troubling her, what does she think is causing Lucretia's mood?

   _____

   _____

6. Contrast the two women, Lucretia Burns and Lily Graham, the teacher.

   _____

   _____

7. In one word, what does the radical Radbourn think that people like himself and Lily should "preach" to the farmers?

   _____

8. How does Lily persuade Lucretia to try again?

   _____

   _____

A New England Nun

Mary E. Wilkins Freeman

Easy

SYNOPSIS

Louisa Ellis, a spinster, lives alone serenely and happily. Now she is about to marry Joe Dagget, recently returned from Australia where he had gone to make his fortune. Their engagement had begun fourteen years ago, before Joe went away; now they are attempting to go on as if there had been no interruption. However, Louisa has become "set in her ways," and is secretly a little uncomfortable when Joe is in her parlor. Joe is uneasy, too, and has the further complication of having fallen in love with Lily Dyer, the woman who takes care of his mother. Yet he remains loyal to Louisa. Louisa overhears a conversation, realizes that Joe and Lily are in love, and rejects Joe gently, making everybody happy.

SUGGESTION

All three characters in this short story have a strong sense of duty. Ask the students to make a list of incidents that show how Louisa, Joe, and Lily all are governed by duty. Then ask them to debate whether or not it is a desirable trait.

ANSWER KEY

1. uncomfortable
2. relieved
3. relieved
4. consternation
5. fear
6. fair-looking, capable
7. honor or right
8. a change
9. sadness
10. nunlike

Name: _____

Date: _____

A New England Nun

One or two well-chosen adjectives or nouns will answer each of the following questions.

1. _____ How does Joe feel when he sits in Louisa's parlor?

2. _____ How does he feel after leaving Louisa's house?

3. _____ How does she feel?

4. _____ When Joe returned after fourteen years, what was Louisa's first emotion?

5. _____ When Joe suggests that Caesar should be set loose, what is Louisa's reaction?

6. _____ How does Louisa describe Lily Dyer?

7. _____ What qualities is Lily Dyer talking about when she says, "I'd never think anything of a man who went against 'em for me or any other girl"?

8. _____ When she rejects Joe, what does Louisa say she is reluctant to make or have?

9. _____ What emotion touches Louisa lightly when Joe leaves?

10. _____ What adjective describing Louisa is suggested in the title and also in the final sentence of the short story?

The Bride Comes to Yellow Sky

Stephen Crane   *Easy*

SYNOPSIS

A train is speeding across Texas, bringing two people (married that morning in San Antonio) to Yellow Sky where the man, Jack Potter, is town marshal. As they near their destination, Potter begins to worry about what effect his surprise marriage will have on his friends, and he dreads meeting them. When they get off the train, the town seems deserted. They hurry toward Potter's house, hoping to meet no one. (Actually, everyone is indoors because Scratchy Wilson, an old "gunslinger," is drunk and roaming the streets, looking for a fight.) As Potter and his bride come around a corner, they are face-to-face with Scratchy, the marshal's enemy. Scratchy, ready to settle old scores with his gun, is at first unbelieving when the marshal says he is unarmed, but when Potter explains that he is returning with his bride, Scratchy slinks off, defeated.

SUGGESTION

This story can be used effectively to demonstrate the advantages of third-person narrative. The omniscient or all-knowing author describes the Potters' wedding morning on the train and then takes his readers to Yellow Sky and the Weary Gentleman Saloon to show what is happening there at the same time. Finally, he arranges the confrontation which the readers are already anticipating. You might ask the students if they think the story would be as effective if it were told in the first person by Jack Potter.

ANSWER KEY

1. had been a cook
2. received a silver watch as a gift
3. an amused and superior grin
4. a target for Scratchy Wilson
5. a maroon-colored flannel shirt
6. trying to sneak up on him
7. shot Wilson in the leg
8. the last of the old gang that used to hang out along the river
9. was talkative and a storyteller
10. a hangdog air
11. the town marshal
12. a brass band
13. blue cashmere and velvet
14. new black clothes
15. the bridegroom

Reading Quiz:

Recalling the Details

Name: _____

Date: _____

The Bride Comes to Yellow Sky

Use the appropriate phrase from Column B to complete each statement in Column A.

Column A

1. The bride _____ . (4 words)

2. The bride _____

   _____ . (7 words)

3. The Negro porter wore _____ . (5 words)

4. The bartender's dog was _____ . (5 words)

5. Scratchy Wilson wore _____ . (4 words)

6. Scratchy Wilson accused Potter of _____

   _____ . (6 words)

7. Jack Potter once _____ . (5 words)

8. Scratchy Wilson was _____

   _____ . (14 words)

9. The drummer in the bar _____

   _____ . (6 words)

10. When Jack Potter got off the train, he had _____ . (3 words)

11. Jack Potter was _____ . (3 words)

12. Yellow Sky had _____ . (3 words)

13. The bride wore _____ . (4 words)

14. Jack Potter wore _____ . (3 words)

15. Jack Potter was _____ . (2 words)

(continued)

150 Great Short Stories

The Bride Comes to Yellow Sky (continued)

Column B

new black clothes

an amused and superior grin

had been a cook

received a silver watch as a gift

blue cashmere and velvet

a brass band

the town marshal

a hangdog air

was talkative and a storyteller

shot Wilson in the leg

a maroon-colored flannel shirt

a target for Scratchy Wilson

trying to sneak up on him

the last of the old gang that used to hang out along the river

the bridegroom

A Leader of the People

John Steinbeck   Moderate

SYNOPSIS

Jody and his parents live on a ranch. He has great respect for the middle-aged ranch hand, Billie Buck, who is both wise and sensitive while Jody's father is stern and somewhat impatient. When a letter comes from Jody's grandfather announcing a visit, his parents argue. His father has no patience with the old man's often-repeated stories about wagon trains and Indians. The first evening doesn't go well; Jody's father shows his indifference while Jodie and Billie Buck urge Grandfather to tell his stories. The next morning, Grandfather explains why the stories are important: "A group of people carried life out here (the West) and set it down," and Grandfather was their leader.

SUGGESTION

Steinbeck makes a point that at least one historian made before him—that there are no more frontiers to conquer in our country, that the "Westering" spirit has died out in the people. Ask the students to arrive at a group definition of that "Westering" spirit before they decide whether or not it still exists. Are there now other kinds of frontiers? (For example, space travel.)

ANSWER KEY

1. He may be bored, or jealous of what the old man has accomplished.

2. He's self-important.

3. He wanted to be the bearer of the news himself.

4. Yes; it was the most important thing in his life and didn't last long enough.

5. to show his interest in the period Grandfather knows best

6. They lack imagination and the yen to cross new frontiers.

A *Leader of the People*

Answer each of the following in a brief, carefully worded sentence.

1. Why do you think Jody's father is so impatient with Grandfather's stories?

   _____

   _____

2. What does the fact that Carl insists on being asked permission before anything is done on the ranch show about him?

   _____

   _____

3. Why does Carl call his son "Big Britches" and seem angry when he finds out that Jody had already told his mother about the letter?

   _____

   _____

4. Does Jody's mother understand why her father talks so much about Indians and wagon trains? Explain.

   _____

   _____

5. Why does Billie Buck mention the powder horn and pistol to Grandfather?

   _____

   _____

6. Why do you think Grandfather says that "Westering" has died out in the new generation of his people? What does he mean?

   _____

   _____

The Hiltons' Holiday

Sarah Orne Jewett   *Easy*

SYNOPSIS

John Hilton, a hardworking farmer, and his wife are sitting outside on a spring evening, waiting for their young daughters, Katy and Susan Ellen, to come home from visiting the new teacher. John, affectionate and boyish, has decided to take his daughters with him to Topham, ostensibly to buy seeds and a hoe, but actually to give the children an outing. His practical wife fears that going to town may give them "notions," but finally agrees to the holiday although she can't be persuaded to go along. The all-day trip is a great success for the girls, not only because of the chance to shop and "see the sights," but also because they have a very special time with their father.

SUGGESTION

"The Hiltons' Holiday" is a good example of the "local color" story. In this case, the setting is rural Maine. Point out to the students how carefully the locality, the people's dress, and their habits are described, and how the dialect lets the reader know how these people spoke. It might be worthwhile also to point out to the students that while Jewett recreated rural New England for her readers, Bret Harte described the frontier mining towns in his stories so that Easterners could imagine what they were like.

ANSWER KEY

1. Topham

2. the Judge's house

3. Topham Academy

4. Judge Masterson

5. John Hilton

6. Mrs. Hilton

7. Katy

8. Susan Ellen

9. the new teacher

10. John Hilton's mother

Name: _____

Date: _____

The Hiltons' Holiday

Below are the descriptions of people or places mentioned in the short story. You are to supply the name of the person or place described.

1. _____ The town which was the Hiltons' destination.

2. _____ A "beautiful old white house standing behind its green trees and terraces and lawns."

3. _____ It had a belfry and "a long row of windows" in the front.

4. _____ He was a courtly old man who had known John Hilton's mother.

5. _____ He was a hardworking farmer who still had boyish enthusiasm.

6. _____ She wanted a new pepper box and didn't want her husband to waste money on "Kickshaws."

7. _____ She was her father's favorite, shy and sensitive, "a real little farmer."

8. _____ She was her mother's favorite, a bit impatient, but eager to help around the house.

9. _____ She gave a party for the children. She promised Katy "some pieces for her doll."

10. _____ Her maiden name was Catherine Winn. She was a fine scholar who attended Topham Academy.

Homesickness

George Moore   *Easy*

<u>SYNOPSIS</u>

After thirteen years in New York, Bryden goes back to Ireland to regain his health. Once there, he notices that the village and countryside now have a rundown look. He rents a loft room in Mike Scully's house and listens to the neighbors who come to talk to the American and tell their tales of woe. Gradually his health improves, and his days are less lonely because he is seeing Margaret Dirken. They are about to be married when a letter from New York makes Bryden homesick once more, and he returns to the States. Only in old age does he go back in dreams to Ireland and Margaret.

<u>SUGGESTION</u>

Ask the students what they think is the main idea (theme) of this story. They should see that Moore is saying that the land of our dreams is far removed from reality: Bryden returned to find his idealized Ireland and, of course, was disappointed. Lonely for New York, he returned and made a life for himself, but still harbored a dream of an Ireland that no longer existed.

ANSWER KEY

1. wants to see it again, and for his health

2. They need cultivation or care; there is an air of desolation.

3. depressing

4. leave the place

5. because she says it is unsuitable for them to be "keeping company"

6. surprise and anger

7. America

8. a letter from the other barman

9. No.

10. when he is an old man

Name: _____

Date: _____

Homesickness

Answer each of the following questions in the fewest possible words.

1. _____ What are Bryden's two reasons for returning to Ireland?

2. _____ How are the countryside and the village different from the way he remembered them?

3. _____ In one word, how did the villagers' talk seem to Bryden?

4. _____ As he lies in his loft bed that first night, what does he wish he could do?

5. _____ Why do you think Bryden suggests marriage to Margaret?

6. _____ What is Bryden's reaction to the people's humble obedience to the priest?

7. _____ Since he grew up among them, he must have behaved the same way once. What has changed him?

8. _____ What "voice from the past" calls Bryden back to New York?

9. _____ When he leaves for the United States, does Margaret expect to see him again?

10. _____ When does Bryden begin to long to see Margaret and Ireland again?

The Wind and the Snow of Winter

Walter Van Tilburg Clark

Easy

SYNOPSIS

Near sunset of an early-winter day, Mike Braneen is coming into Gold Rock with his burro, Annie. For many years he has prospected, and as he walks he is reliving memories. Some are of the burros, eighteen or twenty of them, who were his working companions; some, of the girls he once knew; and some—as it is getting dark and the wind and snow strike his face—of God. He anticipates how pleasant his first night in Gold Rock will be. But when he arrives, the Lucky Boy Saloon is closed; the owner, his old friend, is dead, a stranger tells him. Mrs. Wright's boarding house is gone too. Mike, uncertain and confused, asks no more questions.

SUGGESTION

If students have not already learned the term *symbolism*, this short story is a good one to illustrate it. You could explain that a symbol is something that does exist (the wind and snow of early winter actually strike Mike's face) but also suggests or means something else. (Here, the wind and snow symbolize old age and approaching death.) Students may be able to find other symbols in the story—the lights of the town, for example.

ANSWER KEY

1. prospecting with only a mule for company
2. Highway Dept. employees, mining engineers, travelers
3. cars make him nervous, fears for the safety of his burro
4. a prostitute
5. Armandy
6. makes him think of God
7. lights are not as bright as they used to be
8. The Lucky Boy Saloon is closed.
9. thinks Mike wants a hand-out
10. recognizes Mike, who is probably a legend in town

Reading Quiz:

A Glimpse of the Past

Name: _____

Date: _____

The Wind and the Snow of Winter

Answer briefly.

1. _____   What has been Mike Braneen's life work?

2. _____   When he goes into Gold Rock now, who are the men in the hotel dining room?

3. _____   Why doesn't Mike take the paved road into town?

4. _____   What is the only kind of woman Mike has known?

5. _____   Which one does he remember best?

6. _____   What effect does a sunset have on Mike?

7. _____   What is different about Gold Rock when he finally sees its lights?

8. _____   What is his first shock when he reaches the main street?

9. _____   Why is the stranger a bit unfriendly at first?

10. _____   What changes his attitude?

Neighbour Rosicky

Willa Cather   *Moderate*

SYNOPSIS

Rosicky, a Czech immigrant-farmer, has just been told by his friend, Dr. Burleigh, that his heart is no longer strong enough for farm work and that he must let his sons take over. The doctor is fond of the Rosickys, who are not the area's most prosperous farmers but certainly among the happiest and most generous. Only one of Rosicky's sons, Rudolph, is married, to a town girl, Polly, who thinks farm life is dull. Polly finds an unexpected ally in her father-in-law. She is alone with him when his heart attack comes, and she realizes "that nobody, not her mother, not Rudolph, or anyone really loved her as much as old Rosicky did," for he had the gift of love.

SUGGESTION

"Neighbour Rosicky" is effective characterization, but it is also a short story with a theme or main idea that students can recognize. Ask them what quality of Rosicky's makes him memorable and what truth his life demonstrates. In general, they should see that Rosicky is generous and loving and that a loving person makes life better for everyone with whom she or he comes in contact.

ANSWER KEY

1. They work hard, but take time to enjoy life along the way.

2. He couldn't afford it.

3. Enjoy life; don't try too hard to scrimp and save.

4. He had lived on a farm as a young boy.

5. He wants his married son to use it to take his wife to town.

6. Rosicky took his family on a picnic.

7. He tries to clear the thistles out of the alfalfa.

Name: _____

Date: _____

Neighbour Rosicky

Answer each question in one brief, well-worded sentence.

1. In the opinion of Rosicky's neighbors, why don't he and his boys "get on faster"?

   _____

   _____

2. Why didn't Rosicky buy land on the High Prairie?

   _____

   _____

3. Mary Rosicky and her husband have the same philosophy of life.* What is it?

   _____

   _____

4. What influence from Anton Rosicky's childhood eventually made him tire of cities?

   _____

   _____

5. Why does Rosicky refuse his sons the car for their regular Saturday night trip to the movies?

   _____

   _____

6. What story does Mary tell about the time the corn all dried up in the hot wind on the fourth of July?

   _____

   _____

7. How does Rosicky finally disobey doctor's orders and bring on his heart attack?

   _____

   _____

* Their refusal to sell their cream should give you one clue.

The Widder Johnsing

Ruth McEnery Stuart   *Easy*

SYNOPSIS

Jake Johnson is dead and his widow is going "f'om fits ter convulsions." Sister Temperance has taken charge, consoling the widow and laying out the deceased. Jake's aged parents and his first wife, whom he deserted, are the first people allowed into the inner room to pay their respects. The mourners' sympathy is more with the first wife and her little son than with the new widow, Lize Ann, for she has already buried two husbands and, between marriages, has had "flings" with a number of the married and single men present. But this time, Lize Ann does not run true to form and keeps entirely to herself except for receiving solace from the young minister who, before he knows what happened, is husband number four.

SUGGESTION

This short story, published in 1893, is a good example of Stuart's skill in reproducing the dialect of the Southern-plantation blacks, but it is also effective description of now outmoded customs, particularly the wake. Ask the students to describe rituals in the story that were unfamiliar to them. It might also be worthwhile to ask them whether or not the dialect added to the story's effect.

ANSWER KEY

1. fits and faints
2. three
3. fainted into Pete Richard's arms
4. flirt
5. She keeps to herself.
6. stays after the meeting to talk to the minister
7. had food prepared and two potatoes baked
8. rolls over in laughter
9. tells him he shouldn't come anymore
10. They turn their backs.

The Widder Johnsing

Answer each of the following in the fewest possible words.

1. _____ What are the outward signs of the Widder's grief during the wake and at the funeral?

2. _____ When the story opens, how many times has she been married?

3. _____ What action of Lize Ann's (the Widder) at the funeral caused some speculation among her neighbors?

4. _____ What was Lize Ann apt to do between husbands?

5. _____ How is her behavior different this time?

6. _____ How does she finally arrange to receive "spiritual solace"?

7. _____ What indication is there that she intended to bring a visitor home with her?

8. _____ After the Reverend Langford leaves her cabin the first time, what does the sorrowing widow do?

9. _____ How does she maneuver the Reverend into proposing?

10. _____ What is the reaction of the young single women when Lize Ann turns to receive their congratulations?

UNIT 8

THE VALUES WE CHERISH

Stories of Faith, Courage, Loyalty, and Generosity

UNIT 8

THE VALUES WE CHERISH

The Rat Trap Man

Selma Lagerhöf   *Easy*

SYNOPSIS

Long ago in Sweden, a poor rat trap seller stole money from a cottager who had given him a bed for the night. The next night, seeking shelter at a forge, he is taken home by the ironmaster, who thinks he recognizes him as an old friend who has now come down in the world. When the ironmaster realizes his mistake, his grown daughter insists that they still give the man a Christmas. The next day father and daughter go to church, where they hear about the robbery, and the girl is dejected. But when they return home, the rat trap man is gone, leaving her a rat trap, the stolen money, and a letter thanking her for her kindness and trust.

SUGGESTION

Ask the students to state in one sentence the idea they think the story illustrates. Lagerhöf wants the reader to see that the beggar's theory (the world is a rat trap; the people, victims) came out of his bitterness. The girl's trust and kindness restored his faith in himself and others.

ANSWER KEY

1. A	11. E
2. B	12. C
3. B	13. A
4. A	14. D
5. E	15. D
6. D	16. D
7. D	17. A
8. A	18. E
9. A	19. A
10. E	20. A

Name: _____

Date: _____

The Rat Trap Man

Match the descriptions in Column A with the characters in Column B.

Column A

1. _____ Couldn't earn enough money to get along

2. _____ Boasted about how much money his cow had earned for him

3. _____ Was lonely and eager to talk to someone

4. _____ Was disillusioned and saw the world as a big rat trap

5. _____ Threatened to call the sheriff

6. _____ Suspected that the stranger had stolen or had escaped from jail

7. _____ Was compassionate

8. _____ Didn't want to undeceive the other man all at once

9. _____ Had his faith in human beings and his self-respect restored

10. _____ Thought the stranger was his old friend

11. _____ Was determined to produce good iron

12. _____ Was too haughty to speak to the poor stranger

13. _____ Got lost in the forest

14. _____ Was dejected at the news of the robbery

15. _____ Didn't think the stranger acted like an educated man

16. _____ Interceded for the stranger

17. _____ Did nothing but sleep

18. _____ Was angry because he had mistaken the stranger for someone else

19. _____ Was amazed by Edla's kindness

20. _____ Left Edla a present that made her joyful

Column B

A. the rat trap man

B. the crofter

C. the master blacksmith

D. Edla Willmansson

E. her father, the ironmaster

Tennessee's Partner

Bret Harte   *Easy*

SYNOPSIS

"Tennessee's Partner" was the only name he was known by in Sandy Bar. Short, stout, and unimposing, he made far less impression on his fellow miners than did his flamboyant partner. He'd been married briefly, but his wife soon transferred her affections to Tennessee, and they went off together. When Tennessee returned (the woman had found someone else), the partnership went on as before. Then Tennessee's misbehavior became too much even for Sandy Bar. He was being tried, but no one had any doubt that he'd be hanged. His partner tried to save him, and when that failed, gave Tennessee a proper burial. He died not long after, and Sandy Bar had little doubt that he went to join his old partner.

SUGGESTION

In this short story, Harte develops one of his favorite themes—that a rough exterior often hides such virtues as selflessness, loyalty, and compassion. Tennessee's partner was a nondescript man. Ask the students what special quality (his unswerving loyalty) eventually earned him everyone's respect. You might also ask them to name some of the ways in which that loyalty was demonstrated.

ANSWER KEY

1. shootout
2. get him into trouble; tempt a thief
3. gambler's or poker
4. all his money
5. bribe
6. claim the body
7. attempt to do right by Tennessee
8. brought Tennessee home
9. kindness
10. Tennessee coming to meet him

Name: _____

Date: _____

Tennessee's Partner

Complete each statement with the fewest possible words.

_____ 1. When Tennessee returned after his fling with his partner's wife, everyone expected that there would be a _____ .

_____ 2. Tennessee has a sense of humor, as shown when he robbed a stranger of his knife, pistol, and money, and told him that the first two might _____ and the last might _____ .

_____ 3. When Tennessee was finally cornered, he used a _____ term to surrender.

_____ 4. When Tennessee was being tried, his partner offered _____ to save him.

_____ 5. That offer worked against Tennessee, for the judge considered it a _____ .

_____ 6. Tennessee's partner didn't attend the hanging, but he was waiting to _____ .

_____ 7. The men joined the funeral procession half curiously and half in fun, but finally they were impressed by Tennessee's partner's _____ .

_____ 8. In his eulogy, Tennessee's partner talked about the many times he'd _____ .

_____ 9. The event changed people's attitude toward Tennessee's partner; they began to treat him with _____ .

_____ 10. When Tennessee's partner died, he had a vision of _____ .

The Outcasts of Poker Flat

Bret Harte   *Easy*

<u>SYNOPSIS</u>

Driven out of Poker Flat by "virtuous" citizens, a gambler, two prostitutes, and a petty thief are crossing the mountains to Sandy Bar, a town less critical of its citizens' occupations. A severe snowstorm catches them halfway, along with an innocent young couple who had intended to elope to Poker Flat. True to form, Uncle Billy, the thief, makes off with the horses, and the others are marooned for a week in their log-cabin shelter on very short rations. "Mother Shipton," the older prostitute, shows remarkable generosity before she dies; Oakhurst, the gambler, is their resourceful leader. But nature is cruel in this case, and only the young groom-to-be survives.

<u>SUGGESTION</u>

Bret Harte's favorite theme was that a rough or unlikely exterior often concealed a heart of gold. If you ask the students how this theme is demonstrated in "The Outcasts of Poker Flat," they should be able to point out incidents that reveal Oakhurst's and the prostitutes' selflessness, tenderness, and heroism.

ANSWER KEY

1. B
2. C
3. D
4. E
5. A
6. C
7. F
8. D

9. E
10. C
11. B
12. E
13. B, F
14. C
15. A, C, D, F

Name: _____

Date: _____

The Outcasts of Poker Flat

Match the descriptions in Column A with the names of the characters in Column B.

Column A

1. _____ A waitress at the Temperance House; now she is about to be married

2. _____ A gambler with a kind heart

3. _____ A woman with a bad reputation who shows motherly interest in one of the others marooned in the cabin

4. _____ A young man who once lost $40 to the gambler

5. _____ A drunk and ne'er-do-well who left the others in a predicament

6. _____ The non-drinker among the outcasts

7. _____ The gambler kissed her before he left forever

8. _____ She starved herself to save her rations for someone else

9. _____ He entertained the others with stories from *The Iliad.*

10. _____ He hid away his cards along with the whiskey.

11. _____ She played the accordion to entertain the others.

12. _____ He went off to Poker Flat to bring help.

13. _____ They died in each other's arms.

14. _____ Having done everything he could to help the others, he went off into the snow and shot himself.

15. _____ They were the outcasts (4 names) of Poker Flat.

Column B

A. Uncle Billy

B. Piney Woods

C. John Oakhurst

D. Mother Shipton

E. Tom Simson

F. The Duchess

Thank You, M'am

Langston Hughes

Easy

SYNOPSIS

A boy attempts to snatch a large woman's purse, but bungles the job—he loses his balance and falls down. The woman kicks him, picks him up, and shakes him before ordering him to return her purse. Then she drags him home with her, makes him wash his face, and asks him why he tried to steal. When he says he wanted to buy some suede shoes, she doesn't scold. She makes a meal for the two of them and, when they have finished eating, gives him $10 to buy the shoes. She warns him not to try to steal again. The boy wants to say "Thank you, M'am" when he leaves, but no words will come out.

SUGGESTION

"Thank you, M'am" is a remarkable characterization of Mrs. Luella Bates Washington Jones. Ask the students to review what she says and what she does; then have a brainstorming session to find adjectives that best describe her.

ANSWER KEY

1. Mrs. Luella Bates Washington Jones
2. Roger
3. 11 p.m.
4. purse
5. fell down
6. the thief
7. wash his face, comb his hair
8. suede shoes
9. their supper
10. go to the store
11. hotel beauty shop
12. $10, shoes
13. behave himself
14. "Thank you, M'am"

Thank You, M'am

Supply the missing words to complete each of the following statements.

_____ 1. The victim's name was _____ .

_____ 2. The thief's name was _____ .

_____ 3. The time was _____ .

_____ 4. The thief tried to steal the victim's _____ .

_____ 5. Instead, he _____ .

_____ 6. The victim took _____ home.

_____ 7. She made him _____ and _____ .

_____ 8. When she asked him why he stole, he said he wanted to get some _____ .

_____ 9. She then prepared _____ .

_____ 10. He offered to _____ .

_____ 11. She told him that she worked in a _____ .

_____ 12. When he was leaving, she gave him _____ for the _____ .

_____ 13. When they parted, she told him to _____ .

_____ 14. When he left, he wanted to say _____ , but he wasn't able.

An Underground Episode

Edmund Ware   *Moderate*

SYNOPSIS

Because the trench-digging machine is broken down, two men and a seventeen-year-old boy have spent this cold, rainy Sunday trying to uncover the open end of a newly laid line of sewer pipe. They need to seal it against oozing mud which, left alone, will obstruct it completely. Now, oncoming darkness, the rain and the mud are defeating them. In desperation, they call out the foreman and regular crew to help finish the digging. When the pipe is finally uncovered, the foreman wants a volunteer to crawl through to the manhole, dragging a rope which can then be used to draw sandbags through and clear the pipe. Ashamed of being afraid, the seventeen-year-old volunteers for the task and completes it, but his greatest achievement is conquering his fear.

SUGGESTION

Ware makes two points. First, in order to measure up we sometimes conceal our fear and act courageously. In doing so, we may lose our fear and find the courage we have been feigning. Second, even a small amount of encouragement from another person or evidence that the person believes in us is sometimes all we need to surmount an obstacle. In a discussion, students might be able to illustrate these points from their own experience. Two other literature selections in which students may find parallels to "An Underground Episode" are *The Red Badge of Courage* by Stephen Crane and "The Tuft of Flowers" by Robert Frost.

ANSWER KEY

1. B	6. L	11. E, A
2. G, J	7. D	12. N
3. I	8. D	13. C
4. K	9. M	
5. H	10. F	

Name: _____

Date: _____

An Underground Episode

Complete each statement in Column A with the appropriate word or phrase from Column B. Note that some statements in Column A will require two selections from Column B.

Column A

_____ 1. Three people were digging "the crater" by hand because of _____ .

_____ 2. It was not possible to flush out the pipe with a hose because there was no _____ within _____ .

_____ 3. Because it was _____ , most of the crew were in the shanty.

_____ 4. _____ dreamed of going back to the old country to see his wife and child.

_____ 5. The foreman's name was _____ .

_____ 6. Fifty dollars was the reward for crawling _____ .

_____ 7. _____ picked up the boy and carried him out of the manhole.

_____ 8. _____ called out "Are you all right, kid?" and gave the boy the courage and hope to go on.

_____ 9. At one point during the ordeal, the boy had only _____ clearance.

_____ 10. Almost without knowing that he was doing it, the boy began counting _____ during his ordeal.

_____ 11. While the men were digging, rain, _____ and _____ made their job difficult.

_____ 12. Toward the end, the _____ was the boy's only incentive to keep going.

_____ 13. Everyone but the boy realized he was the only one who could crawl through because of the pipe's _____ .

Column B

A. cold

B. the digger's broken pistol

C. narrowness

D. Alamo Laska

E. mud

F. joints

G. water plug

H. Stender

I. Sunday

J. a mile

K. Nick Christopher

L. 300 feet

M. 2 inches

N. light

Jacob

Jack Schaefer   *Moderate*

SYNOPSIS

The narrator, an elderly man, tells of his boyhood in a small Montana town of the 1870's where his father was a switchman for the railroad. Talk of Indians fired the boy's imagination, but he never saw a brave until he met Jacob, a Nez Percé chief. Jacob's small band of followers, having resisted the U.S. Cavalry as long as possible, was now being taken by train to an Indian reservation. In the narrator's town, the train was shunted to a siding to let the night freight pass. While his father was setting switches, the narrator stepped aboard the train and witnessed an encounter between Jacob and a drunken soldier who tried to kill the chief, but the boy intervened. Jacob later rewards his "friend" by sending a pair of chief's moccasins.

SUGGESTION

You might point out that first-person narrative gives the story authenticity and makes the reader feel as if the narrator is speaking directly to him or her about a personal experience. Students could be asked to list clues that reveal the narrator's age and what details make this fiction seem like a true story.

ANSWER KEY

1. "The only good Indian is a dead Indian."

2. the attitude of his father and other men

3. Nez Percé land was being taken.

4. Winter was coming; his people were dying.

5. He respects Jacob.

6. recognizes Jacob's nobility; sees the Indians as tired, defeated, old

7. that he is leaving all that is good and free for captivity

Name: _____

Date: _____

Jacob

A carefully worded sentence is sufficient to answer each of the following questions. Your answers will show how well you understood the significance of this short story.

1. Before his encounter with Jacob, what was the boy's attitude toward Indians?

   _____

   _____

2. What had formed that attitude?

   _____

   _____

3. What was the reason for the skirmishes between Jacob's Nez Percé followers and the U.S. Cavalry?

   _____

   _____

4. Why did Jacob finally surrender?

   _____

   _____

5. What attitude toward Jacob does the captain in charge of the Indian train hold?

   _____

   _____

6. How does the narrator's attitude toward Indians change in the course of the story?

   _____

   _____

7. As the boy watches Jacob "looking far down the track" toward the distant horizon, what does he surmise that Jacob is thinking?

   _____

   _____

Scars of Honor

Dorothy Johnson

Moderate

SYNOPSIS

When the old Indian, Charley Lockjaw, died, four young Indians sacrificed a valuable horse on his grave, to the surprise of the white ranchers and the Indian agent. But to those making the sacrifice, Charley was their link to the glorious past. He had led them through a ritual test of endurance before they went off to enlist during World War II. Although they had passed his test, two were actually rejected for the service. One was his lame grandson, Joe. The other, Tom Little Hand, was eventually called up despite his poor eyesight. When word came out that Tom was wounded, Joe wanted to make a sacrifice to help Tom get well. The ritual Charley taught him was a painful one that gave him his "scars of honor."

SUGGESTION

In this story, Johnson effectively contrasts the present-day lifestyle of the Indians with their traditional one. Ask the students to list some of those contrasts. (For example, now the people don't bathe much; long ago, they bathed daily, even if they had to break the ice in the river to do it.) In a discussion, students might try to enumerate the influences that have caused the changes.

ANSWER KEY

1. E
2. D
3. B
4. A
5. I

6. J
7. G
8. H
9. C
10. F

Reading Quiz: Name: _____

Understanding the Characters   Date: _____

Scars of Honor

Complete each of the following statements in Column A by choosing the appropriate phrase or clause from Column B.

Column A

_____ 1. Charley Lockjaw had to be secretive about performing the ceremonies because _____ .

_____ 2. To help his friend who was wounded, Joe wanted his grandfather to teach him _____ .

_____ 3. The Indians were eager to enlist because _____ .

_____ 4. In the old days, a brave won glory if he showed_____ .

_____ 5. If Charley Lockjaw had lived in an earlier time, he would have been treated with respect because _____ .

_____ 6. The young men wanted Charley to teach them the ceremony of the dream on the hilltop because _____ .

_____ 7. In World War I, the Indians were not asked to fight because _____ , but many did anyway.

_____ 8. Traditionally, if a warrior carried a sacred buffalo shield, he was _____ .

_____ 9. Charley Lockjaw was ashamed of the girls who hung around the soldiers because in the old days _____ .

_____ 10. The boys sacrificed the horse on Charley's grave because he would need it as _____ .

Column B

A. courage in the face of death

B. fighting was part of their tradition

C. Cheyennes could take pride in the virtue of their women

D. the ceremony for swinging at the pole

E. the old religion had been outlawed by the government in Washington

F. he went along the Hanging Road

G. they were not citizens

H. pledged not to retreat

I. he was old and wise

J. they were going to war

184   *150 Great Short Stories*

Sheener

Ben Ames Williams   *Easy*

SYNOPSIS

The narrator, a newspaperman, recalls the Jewish newsboy, Sheener, who worked in his office and befriended the second assistant janitor, who called himself Evans. Everyone else saw Evans as a bum and a drunk, but Sheener was certain he was a "gent," down on his luck. Sheener did Evans's work when he was off on a spree, interceded for him when the narrator would have fired him, and eventually, when alcohol had destroyed Evans's health, took care of him and engineered a reunion with Evans's wealthy son. As a reward, Evans snubbed Sheener, apparently because he didn't want the son to know he had associated with such a low-class person.

SUGGESTION

The story of Sheener offers a good opportunity for a classroom debate on the topic, "Clothes make the man." If only one student or a few students have read the story, one can retell "Sheener" so that everyone has enough of the background to relate the general topic to the short story.

ANSWER KEY

1. lofty bearing, aristocratic appearance, hints of his well-to-do family

2. caring (but answers will vary)

3. had the D.T.'s and was close to death; didn't want a pauper's burial

4. He is sober and wants to be well groomed.

5. Sheener (but answers may vary)

Reading Quiz:
A Closer Look

Name: _____

Date: _____

Sheener

Answer each of the following questions in one carefully worded sentence.

1. What about Evans's appearance or behavior convinced Sheener that the janitor was really a "gent"?

   _____

   _____

2. What one adjective would you use to describe Sheener's attitude toward Evans? Explain why you chose that word.

   _____

   _____

3. What event prompted Evans to reveal his true identity to Sheener? Why did he think it necessary?

   _____

   _____

4. How is Evans affected by the news that his son is coming to see him?

   _____

   _____

5. Who is true gentleman in the story? Explain your choice.

   _____

   _____

150 Great Short Stories

The Bishop's Candlesticks

Victor Hugo

Easy

SYNOPSIS

Released after 19 years in prison, Jean Valjean is sent to a bishop's house for shelter when no one else will let him in. The bishop treats him like an honored guest and calls him brother. Their meal is simple, but the table is set with all the silver they own. In the night, Jean Valjean goes to the bishop's bedroom, stares awhile at the peacefully sleeping old man, then opens the cupboard, steals the silver, and leaves. In the morning, the police come, having caught the ex-convict. The bishop says he gave the silver to Valjean and intended for him to have a pair of silver candlesticks, too; but when the police depart, he counsels Jean Valjean solemnly that now his soul belongs to God.

SUGGESTION

The theme of this short story is important and timeless. Ask students to state in one sentence what important point Hugo makes. They should be able to see that in "The Bishop's Candlesticks" compassion and generosity restored a man's faith and turned him from a life of crime.

ANSWER KEY

1. because he is an ex-convict

2. A kind woman sends him there.

3. Christ

4. to show Jean Valjean that he is an honored and trusted guest

5. Answers will vary.

6. Someone needed it more than he did.

7. to convince them that he had intended for Jean Valjean to have the silver

8. Jean Valjean must use the silver to become an honest man.

Name: _____

Date: _____

The Bishop's Candlesticks

Answer each question in one carefully worded sentence.

1. Why is Jean Valjean turned away wherever he searches for shelter?

   _____

   _____

2. How does he happen to go to the bishop's house?

   _____

   _____

3. When Jean Valjean is overwhelmed and confused by the bishop's kindness, to whom does that good man say the house belongs?

   _____

   _____

4. Why does the bishop want all the silver on the table?

   _____

   _____

5. Do you think Jean Valjean considered killing the bishop? Explain.

   _____

   _____

6. What is the bishop's attitude about the stolen silver?

   _____

   _____

7. With the officers watching, why does he offer Jean Valjean the candlesticks?

   _____

   _____

8. What pact does he make with the ex-convict after the officers leave?

   _____

   _____

All the Young Men

Oliver LaFarge   Moderate

SYNOPSIS

Old Singer, a Navajo medicine man, began to go to pieces after his wife's death. He no longer bothered to collect his fees, spent his money carelessly, and was soon in debt to his friend, the white trader. Then Old Singer went to live with his granddaughter and her husband Wesley, Indians who had forsaken the old ways. Wesley was making a good living selling bootleg liquor to the reservation Indians. Through him, Old Singer became a drunkard. When no one needed him anymore, he wandered away, was picked up by white police, and jailed for drunkenness. In his cell he went into a trance, praying to Slayer of Enemy Gods. He dreamed of all the young warriors he once knew, and just as reality was about to intrude, Old Singer died.

SUGGESTION

In "All the Young Men," LaFarge makes several references to Navajo beliefs and attitudes—for example, the importance of Old Singer's medicine bundle and the Indians' aversion to being in an enclosed space. Students might review the story after they have read it once and list all such references they can find.

ANSWER KEY

1. C		7. G	
2. I		8. F	
3. D		9. K	
4. J		10. A	
5. H		11. E	
6. B		12. J	

All the Young Men

Choose the correct word or phrase from Column A to complete each statement in Column B.

Column A

_____ 1. The most important thing in Old Singer's life is his _____ .

_____ 2. Kit Carson never succeeded in capturing _____ .

_____ 3. In his youth, Old Singer was known as _____ .

_____ 4. Old Singer is finally rescued from a life that has no meaning by _____ .

_____ 5. The man who was breaking the law by bootlegging liquor to the reservation Indians was _____ .

_____ 6. The man who was a friend to Old Singer and knew of his glorious past was _____ .

_____ 7. The husband of Singer's granddaughter persuaded him that liquor would bring _____ .

_____ 8. Singer is disillusioned because many of the Indians have rejected their heritage for _____ .

_____ 9. The brave who had once accompanied Singer on a raid against the Zuni was _____ .

_____ 10. Covering Singer's medicine bundle was _____ .

_____ 11. In his trance in the jail cell, Old Singer's _____ returns.

_____ 12. He prays to _____ .

Column B

A. a perfect buckskin

B. the trader

C. religion

D. Hasty Arrow

E. youth

F. White Man's ways

G. beautiful mystical experience

H. Wesley

I. Haskinini's men

J. Slayer of Enemy Gods

K. Hurries to War

UNIT 9

CHILLERS AND THRILLERS ====

Stories of Mystery, Murder, and the Supernatural

Unit 9

Chillers and Thrillers
Stories of Mystery, Murder, and the Supernatural 191

The Cask of Amontillado

Edgar Allan Poe

Easy

SYNOPSIS

Montresor, insulted by Fortunato, vows revenge. During the carnival, he meets Fortunato and invites him back to his palazzo to judge a recently purchased cask of Amontillado. He knows Fortunato considers himself an authority on wine and will accept readily. No servants are in the house; Montresor has seen to that. Carrying torches, the two men descend into the vaults. Fortunato, who has a cold and is slightly drunk, is soon coughing from the dampness. His host gives him wine. They go deeper and deeper into the catacombs. Then, by a ruse, Montresor gets Fortunato into a niche, chains him, and begins to mortar the entrance. Fortunato, suddenly sober, implores his host to free him. Calmly, Montresor sets the final tier of stone in place.

SUGGESTION

Writing on the short story, Poe said in effect that nothing should be included which is not necessary to develop a single incident, that even the opening sentence must be fashioned with this rule in mind. Call to the students' attention that Poe never states what Fortunato's offense against Montresor was—it is not necessary to the story. They should note also that although the story is brief, it is as carefully constructed as was Montresor's plan.

ANSWER KEY

1. In the story, Montresor makes certain that he has revenge for Fortunato's slight.

2. He plans to do some masonry work to bury Fortunato.

3. He knows that Fortunato is soon to die.

4. He knows what the cause of Fortunato's death will be.

5. to torture Fortunato, who cannot free himself

6. Fortunato, buried alive, won't rest in peace.

Reading Quiz: Name: _____

These Words Have Great Significance   Date: _____

The Cask of Amontillado

Answer each of the following in a carefully worded sentence.

1. Relate Montresor's family motto, which translates as "No one attacks me with impunity" (freedom from punishment), to the story.

   _____

   _____

2. Fortunato belongs to the order of Masons; Montresor says he is a mason too. What does he really mean?

   _____

   _____

3. When Fortunato drinks to the dead, Montresor drinks to Fortunato's long life. Why is his toast ironic?

   _____

   _____

4. When Fortunato says that his cough is nothing, that he will not die of a cold, Montresor says, "True, true." What is the significance of his words?

   _____

   _____

5. When he has already chained Fortunato, Montresor says, in part, "Once more let me implore you to return." Why does he say that?

   _____

   _____

6. The final sentence of the short story is the Latin phrase which means "rest in peace." Why is that ironic?

   _____

   _____

Sredni Vashtar

Saki (H.H. Munro)   *Easy*

SYNOPSIS

A sickly, imaginative ten-year-old, Conradin, lives with his guardian, Mrs. De Ropp, a meddling old woman whom he hates. His imaginary world is in the old tool shed at the bottom of the garden where he keeps a hen and, carefully concealed, a ferret. To Conradin, the ferret is a god, Sredni Vashtar, to whom he makes sacrifices and from whom he repeatedly asks one boon. Having decided that Conradin spends too much time in the tool shed, Mrs. De Ropp sells the hen, but still doesn't discover the ferret. Then one day she goes to the shed, determined to find out what its attraction is for Conradin. She never returns.

SUGGESTION

"Sredni Vashtar" is a mixture of fantasy and reality. Ask the students to decide, either in a class discussion or in a theme, whether or not they think Saki wanted his readers to believe that Conradin's boon was granted. Actually, the author gave enough clues for a rational explanation of the tragic accident: Mrs. De Ropp was near-sighted; the shed was dark; ferrets are fierce animals.

ANSWER KEY

1. cousin and guardian
2. imagination
3. hate
4. dislike
5. in the tool shed
6. the hen and the ferret
7. the ferret
8. selling the hen
9. she is nearsighted
10. to destroy his guardian
11. disappeared into the bushes
12. made himself more toast

Name: _____

Date: _____

Sredni Vashtar

Answer each of the following in the fewest possible words. (You won't need more than five words per answer.)

1. _____ What is Mrs. De Ropp's relationship to Conradin?

2. _____ What is the one quality that he possesses that makes the world bearable for Conradin?

3. _____ What emotion does he have toward Mrs. De Ropp?

4. _____ What emotion does she have for him?

5. _____ Where does Conradin spend most of his time?

6. _____ Who are his companions there?

7. _____ Who is Sredni Vashtar?

8. _____ What act of Mrs. De Ropp's, done supposedly "for his own good," angers Conradin?

9. _____ Why didn't Mrs. De Ropp see the ferret when she visited the tool shed the first time?

10. _____ What do you think Conradin asked of Sredni Vashtar?

11. _____ What became of the ferret?

12. _____ What was Conradin's reaction when he heard the maid's scream?

The Boarded Window

Ambrose Bierce   *Difficult*

SYNOPSIS

This grisly incident of the Ohio frontier took place in 1830, but the narrator learned its details from his grandfather. A settler, Murlock, returns to his log cabin in the forest one day to find his young wife ill with a mysterious fever. Three days later, despite his careful nursing, she dies. That night, having prepared her body for burial, he falls into a deep sleep. He is awakened by sounds of a struggle, and fires his rifle into the darkness. Its flash reveals a panther carrying off his wife's body. He faints and wakes once more to daylight—his wife's body now lies near the window, and a fragment of the beast's ear is between her teeth.

SUGGESTION

The conclusion of "The Boarded Window" is so startling that most students are confused at first about what happened; the story is somewhat ambiguous. Obviously, the struggle was between the forces of good and evil, but students will enjoy speculating about the strange cry, the struggle, and the physical evidence that a beast was present. Also, they will want to decide the significance of the boarded window.

ANSWER KEY

1. Answers will vary.

2. Answers will vary.

3. Answers will vary.

4. poverty

5. lack of necessities

6. damage, ruin, devastation

7. pertaining to sorrow for sins

8. filling in the cracks with clay or mortar

9. hermit

10. fearless

Name: _____

Date: _____

The Boarded Window

On first encountering "The Boarded Window," many readers are left feeling a bit confused. Perhaps you were too. In the first three questions of this exercise, you are asked to give your explanation of three events in the log cabin. (There are no right or wrong answers here; simply state briefly what you thought.)

1. How do you account for the cry from the woods which may have come after Murlock fell asleep?

   _____

   _____

2. What do you think struck the table as Murlock leaned on it?

   _____

   _____

3. What did that struggle in the darkness suggest to you?

   _____

   _____

The rest of the quiz may be easier for you, and there are correct answers!

The following words were taken from the story. First, look at each word in context and try to decide its meaning. Write it down, then use a dictionary to verify what you have written.

4. indigence _____

5. privations _____

6. ravage _____

7. penitential _____

8. "chinking" _____

9. recluse _____

10. intrepid _____

Miriam

Truman Capote

Moderate

SYNOPSIS

Mrs. Miller, a widow, meets an odd little girl, Miriam, at the movies one winter evening. A week later, near midnight, Miriam appears at Mrs. Miller's door, invites herself in, and takes command of the situation. Before she leaves, she takes Mrs. Miller's favorite brooch and smashes a vase she dislikes. Two days later, as if by prearrangement, Miriam comes again in the late afternoon and announces she's there to stay. In fact, she has her clothes with her. Terrified, Mrs. Miller runs to a neighbor and, somewhat incoherently, tells her story. But the neighbor's husband can find no trace of the child. Then, when Mrs. Miller is again alone, Miriam comes out of the bedroom to greet her.

SUGGESTION

"Miriam" will generate a lively classroom discussion. Was Mrs. Miller suffering from hallucinations, or was the child a premonition of death? Does Mrs. Miller die at the end of the story?

ANSWER KEY

1. excitement

2. The child's name is the same as her own.

3. hadn't given the girl her address

4. snowy

5. white satin

6. sang even though it was not morning, and the cage was covered

7. a small girl in a bridal gown leading a procession of people down a mountain path

8. white roses, a vase, glazed cherries, almond cake

9. Answers will vary—they think she's crazy, or seeing things.

10. a funeral parlor

11. Answers will vary.

Name: _____

Date: _____

Miriam

Answer each of the following questions in the fewest possible words.

1. _____ What is Mrs. Miller's immediate reaction when she sees Miriam for the first time?

2. _____ What coincidence does Mrs. Miller discover when she asks the child her name?

3. _____ What was especially surprising to Mrs. Miller about the fact that Miriam came to visit?

4. _____ What had the weather been for several days?

5. _____ What color dress was Miriam wearing when she came to visit?

6. _____ What was unusual about the canary's behavior during Miriam's visit?

7. _____ The day after Miriam's visit, what does Mrs. Miller dream?

8. _____ What are Mrs. Miller's purchases when she goes out?

9. _____ After the man searches Mrs. Miller's apartment, what do he and his wife think is the problem?

10. _____ When Mrs. Miller returns to her apartment, of what does it remind her?

11. _____ In your opinion, what finally happens to Mrs. Miller?

Junkie Joe Had Some Money

Ronald Milner   Moderate

SYNOPSIS

The narrator, a fourteen-year-old, recalls a horrible event that took place when he was twelve. The boys in his gang used to taunt an old junkman, Junkie Joe, and the narrator, feeling a little ashamed, went along with the others. Then one winter evening, as he was going home alone, he discovered that the barn where Junkie Joe lived was on fire. He ran to open the barn door, calling out to the junkman, and surprised "two big cats" about to take off after murdering the old man and stealing his money. At first, the boy is certain they will kill him too, but they let him go after threatening him. Now, two years later, they are still a threat, and he begs his parents to move away.

SUGGESTION

This short story can effectively demonstrate point of view. The events are seen through the eyes of a young boy, the narrator. His reactions and his language are what we might expect from a twelve-year-old. Students should see that Milner's use of this technique gives the story immediacy and makes it more believable.

ANSWER KEY

1. says Junkie Joe is really a nice man, keeps his barn house neat and clean; says he "knows better" but goes along with the others

2. He has been seriously ill, and they think he is delirious.

3. nothing else to do for excitement

4. One realizes two murders would cause a stir, but they can make it look as though Junkie Joe died in the fire.

5. He's trying to erase the awful memory.

6. trying to escape his thoughts, felt secure nowhere

Name: _____

Date: _____

Junkie Joe Had Some Money

Answer each of the following questions in one complete sentence.

1. What indication do you have that the narrator is a sensitive boy, but is afraid not to "go along with" the gang?

   _____

   _____

2. When the narrator says that Junkie Joe had some money, why does no one believe him?

   _____

   _____

3. Why did the boys tease Junkie Joe?

   _____

   _____

4. When the narrator surprises the "two big cats" at Junkie Joe's, why don't they kill him too?

   _____

   _____

5. When the narrator describes how he washed his face with snow to get rid of the blood, why does he repeat: "Washed it! Washed it! Washed it!"?

   _____

   _____

6. How do you explain the fact that after Junkie Joe's murder, the boy "just ran and ran," avoiding everyone?

   _____

   _____

Thus I Refute Beelzy

John Collier   *Moderate*

SYNOPSIS

At tea time, Mrs. Carter and her guest, Betty, talk of Small Simon, the Carters' son, who is so engrossed in the solitary game he plays in the garden that he seems oblivious of the bell calling him to tea. By the time the child joins the women, Mr. Carter (Big Simon) arrives, home early because two patients cancelled their appointments. At first, Carter is the enlightened parent, questioning his son about his fantasy playmate, Mr. Beelzy. But soon his patience wears thin and, with threats, he sends the boy to his room. Shortly after, the father goes upstairs too. The women hear a horrible scream—on the second-floor landing, they find what remains of Mr. Carter.

SUGGESTION

The title of this story is particularly well chosen, but students will miss its significance unless they know the meaning of *refute* and realize that *Beelzy* could easily be a shortened form of Beelzebub, the Devil. A bit of dictionary work may be necessary before discussing the aptness of the title. Then they should have no difficulty deciding to whom "I" refers.

ANSWER KEY

1. It is unusual that a small boy would be indifferent to food, strange that he seemed not to hear the bell.

2. This is not normal six-year-old behavior.

3. He seems more mature and older than his parent.

4. He no longer identifies with his parents and the real world.

5. He rejects his family; Mr. Beelzy is now his refuge and security.

Thus I Refute Beelzy

Horror stories often have surprise endings, but if you look over such a story the second time, you may discover that the author gave you a number of clues which you did not notice on your first reading. How was each of the following an indication that something was amiss in the Carter household? (Keep your answers brief, but use complete sentences.) It might be helpful in answering the questions if you try to remember how you, as a six-year-old, might have reacted during the tea-time session.

1. Small Simon was so engaged in "solemn mumbo-jumbo" that he seemed unaware of everything else, including the bell for tea.

   _____

   _____

2. Small Simon would not play with other children, was angry if his mother interrupted his solitary games, and seemed exhausted and nervous when he came in.

   _____

   _____

3. Simon introduces Mr. Beelzy's name and is angry when accused of making him up.

   _____

   _____

4. Simon says he is "not frightened" of Mr. Beelzy, that Mr. Beelzy loves him, and that Mr. Beelzy is "real" while Big Simon and Small Simon are "pretend."

   _____

   _____

5. Small Simon, when threatened by his father, sees Mr. Beelzy as his refuge and protection.

   _____

   _____

The Visitor

Henry Treece   *Moderate*

SYNOPSIS

The young son has been left alone on the farm while all the others, including the laborers and stockmen, have gone to attend market-day. He is contentedly puffing on a cigarette when a strange little old man appears from behind the hedge. The man forces his way into the house and demands food and money, threatening the boy with a long, stiletto-like knife. The boy finally succeeds in knocking him down, but then runs for water, thinking he may have killed him. When he returns, the man has disappeared. The boy runs wildly down the road and meets his returning family. No one quite believes his story until the next morning when the day servant is found in the barn, almost decapitated.

SUGGESTION

This "chiller" has some remarkably effective description. Ask the students to reread the details of the madman's appearance, noting the similes and carefully chosen adjectives. (For example, "eyes rimmed red as a ferret's" and "corpse-grey" skin.)

ANSWER KEY

1. gone to market
2. a strange old man
3. man, his way
4. madman, knife
5. feed, money, lick
6. knocking him
7. water, disappeared
8. the bus with his mother and brother aboard
9. story
10. found murdered

The Visitor

If you complete each of the following statements correctly, you will have summarized the story.

_____ 1. The young narrator is alone on the farm because his family and the employees have _____ .

_____ 2. He is enjoying a forbidden cigarette when from behind the hedge comes _____ .

_____ 3. The _____ forces _____ into the house.

_____ 4. He is obviously a _____ and has a wicked-looking _____ .

_____ 5. He forces the boy to _____ him, give him _____ and _____ his boots.

_____ 6. Finally, the boy succeeds in _____ down.

_____ 7. The boy runs for _____ . When he returns, the man has _____ .

_____ 8. The boy runs down the road and meets _____ .

_____ 9. Everyone doubts his _____ .

_____ 10. Next morning, the day girl, Elsie Hodgson, is _____ .

The Town Where Nobody Got Off

Ray Bradbury   *Easy*

SYNOPSIS

Two salesmen aboard the Chicago-Los Angeles train talk idly of the little towns they are passing, places where no one would ever get off unless he belonged there. On a whim, one of the salesmen decides to get off at the next town, seeking—adventure? Romance? On the station platform he sees no one but an old man sitting idly. All day and evening, as he wanders around the town, the old man is nearby. Finally, they talk, and the old man confesses he has waited 20 years for a stranger, someone he could murder without ever being discovered! But the salesman confesses he harbors the same desire. This strange encounter ends in a draw.

SUGGESTION

Bradbury's shock ending has great impact because the story starts so innocently. Ask the students when they first began to see the old man as a sinister character. Answers will probably vary. There is ambiguity in the ending too. Students could discuss whether or not the salesman is bluffing the old man and give reasons, based on the text, for their decision.

ANSWER KEY

1. otherwise, will always wonder what he missed

2. romance, adventure, thinks he will be disappointed

3. points out that everyone has the desire to kill at times

4. agrees that everyone is a potential killer

5. He is fighting for survival.

6. Each had a sense of waiting for something that was bound to happen.

7. Answers will vary.

The Town Where Nobody Got Off

Answer each of the questions in one carefully worded sentence.

1. Why, in the salesman's words, is it important that he get off the train and visit Rampart Junction?

   _____

   _____

2. What does the other salesman think he is looking for?

   _____

   _____

3. How does the old man attempt to make his weird plan seem reasonable?

   _____

   _____

4. How does the salesman unintentionally make it easier for the old man to explain his plan?

   _____

   _____

5. Why is the salesman so agitated as he tells his problems and explains, "it would do me a world of good"?

   _____

   _____

6. What did the old man and the salesman have in common?

   _____

   _____

7. Do you think the salesman was telling the truth? Explain.

   _____

   _____

The Killers

Ernest Hemingway   *Easy*

SYNOPSIS

Only the counterman, George, and Nick Adams are in the lunchroom when two strangers, hired killers, come in. They are sarcastic and belligerent to George and finally tell him to call in the black cook from the kitchen. One of them, Al, takes the cook and Nick back to the kitchen and ties them up. The other man stays with George, telling him to discourage any stray customers. After an hour's wait for Ole Andreson, the man they plan to kill, they decide he's not coming in, and they leave. George sends Nick to warn Andreson, who already knows they are in town, but can't make up his mind to go out and face them.

SUGGESTION

Ask the students what they notice about Hemingway's style of writing—seemingly simple but actually difficult to imitate. Some of the characteristics they should notice are the clipped, authentic dialogue, the minimum of description, and the short sentences. Ask them to try one paragraph imitating Hemingway. You might have a class vote to see who comes closest to the "real thing."

ANSWER KEY

1. A, B	8. E
2. B	9. F
3. E	10. B
4. F	11. C
5. B	12. A
6. E	13. D
7. B	

Name: _____

Date: _____

The Killers

You probably noticed that "The Killers" has very little description; the dialogue lets you know what kind of person each man is. See if you can identify the speaker in each of the following quotations.

A. Nick Adams
B. George, the counterman
C. Sam, the cook

D. Ole Andreson, the hunted
E. Al, one of the gunmen
F. Max, the other gunman

1. _____   "What's the idea?" (Two people say that at different times; list both.)

2. _____   "What are you going to do to him?" (Al has asked who is out in the kitchen.)

3. _____   "Listen, bright boy, stand a little further along the bar. You move to the left, Max."

4. _____   "We're going to kill a Swede. Do you know a big Swede named Ole Andreson?"

5. _____   "What are you going to kill Ole Andreson for? What did he ever do to you?"

6. _____   "Shut up, you talk too _ _ _ _ _ much."

7. _____   "Sam's gone out. He'll be back in about half an hour."

8. _____   "I don't like it. It's sloppy. You talk too much."

9. _____   "Oh, what the hell. We've got to keep amused, haven't we?"

10. _____   "Listen, you better go see Ole Andreson."

11. _____   "You better not have anything to do with it at all. You better stay way out of it."

12. _____   "I was up Henry's and two fellows came in and tied up me and the cook, and they were going to kill you."

13. _____   "The only thing is, I just can't make up my mind to go out. I been in here all day."

The Tell-Tale Heart

Edgar Allan Poe   *Moderate*

SYNOPSIS

The narrator admits to having been "dreadfully nervous" with heightened sensibilities, but goes on to show that he could not have been mad and planned his crime so carefully. He had nothing against the old man except that he found his pale blue eye disturbing. To get rid of it, he had to kill the man, and for seven nights he prepared. On the eighth night, the deed was done. Afterwards, he dismembered the body and hid the pieces under the floorboards. When the police arrived (the victim's single scream had been reported), all seemed well until the narrator could no longer bear the sound of the old man's heart beating under the floorboards, and he confessed.

SUGGESTION

Students can have a lively discussion trying to decide what really happened in "The Tell-Tale Heart." Was the narrator having hallucinations, or did his guilty conscience make him think he heard the heartbeat? Were the police really fooled, or did they realize that he was deranged and that he would eventually tell them what they wanted to know?

ANSWER KEY

1. because he couldn't stand his pale blue eye

2. by showing how cleverly he planned the murder

3. shutters were closed

4. thinks the old man's heart is beating so loudly that the neighbors will hear

5. the old man's single shriek

6. He himself cried out in a dream.

7. gone to the country

8. hears the old man's heart beating and thinks everyone else must hear it too

The Tell-Tale Heart

Answer each of the following questions in one brief sentence.

1. Why did the narrator kill the old man?

   _____

   _____

2. How does the narrator try to convince his audience that he is not really mad?

   _____

   _____

3. Why was the old man's room so dark?

   _____

   _____

4. What finally agitates the narrator so much that he jumps upon the old man and kills him?

   _____

   _____

5. What do the neighbors hear?

   _____

   _____

6. How does the narrator explain to the police the sound the neighbors heard?

   _____

   _____

7. Where does he tell the police the old man is?

   _____

   _____

8. What makes the narrator confess?

   _____

   _____

UNIT 10

CHILDHOOD MEMORIES ══════════

UNIT 10

CHILDHOOD MEMORIES **213**

The Corvidae
Alwyn Lee
Difficult

SYNOPSIS

As a young boy, the narrator traveled each summer from his home in Melbourne to the Australian "bush" and a sheep ranch owned by his great-uncle Hugh McInstrie. The McInstries, Scottish Presbyterians, are stern, with no sentimental nonsense about them. They consider the narrator a bit puny and sissified because he is interested in birds. One Sunday afternoon, the boy goes to the lambing paddock to watch plovers. He sees them, but also sees a sheep with its eyes pecked out by crows. He manages to slaughter the sheep to put it out of its misery. Next day, the great-uncle shows the boy how to make a crow trap. He catches thirteen crows. His uncle's next instruction, which he obeys, is to go into the trap and beat them to death as a warning to other Corvidae.

SUGGESTION

This short story, with its Australian setting, gives student readers a glimpse of a way of life quite different from their own. Ask them to list on the chalkboard customs, expressions, etc., that were new to them.

ANSWER KEY

1. was an amateur ornithologist, would know Latin names

2. had courage, but was not bloodthirsty

3. "faded" into the "bush"; many died

4. Men were beside the train tracks crying "Paper! Paper!" (newspaper) because they were so eager for the news.

5. indifferent to their beauty, didn't hesitate to slaughter them

6. Answers will vary.

Name: _____

Date: _____

The Corvidae

Use one carefully worded sentence to answer each of the following.

1. *Corvidae* is the Latin name for the crow family. Why do you think Lee called his story "The Corvidae" instead of the "The Crows"? (Clue: Remember what he said about his boyhood interests.)

   _____

   _____

2. In his relatives' opinion, the boy is puny, even sissified. Do you agree? (Clue: Remember the incident of the sheep the crows had maimed.)

   _____

   _____

3. What became of the aborigines when the McInstries began to clear the land for their sheep farm?

   _____

   _____

4. What did the author observe during his twelve-hour train ride that gives some indication of the loneliness and isolation of many people in the "bush"?

   _____

   _____

5. What is the general attitude of the McInstries toward wild creatures—the rabbits, the emu, even the eagle?

   _____

   _____

6. In a sentence, using colorful adjectives, give your impression of the McInstries.

   _____

   _____

A Cap for Steve

Morley Callaghan

Easy

SYNOPSIS

Dave Diamond, a poor laborer, can't understand his twelve-year-old son Steve's preoccupation with baseball when he could be earning a little money. When the Phillies come to town, father and son go to the game. Afterwards, Steve is lucky enough to pick up Eddie Condon's cap when it blows off, and Condon tells the boy to keep it. Suddenly, Steve is a neighborhood celebrity, until someone steals the cap. Later, Steve sees his cap on another boy. In a confrontation, that boy's well-to-do father gives Dave $20 for the cap, but in the process, Dave loses his son's respect. Eventually, out of the incident comes a closer relationship between father and son.

SUGGESTION

"A Cap for Steve" can be a good basis for a class discussion on communication, or the lack of it, between parents and children. Dave Diamond, a practical man, is chiefly concerned with making enough money to support his family. His son, idealistic, longs for his father's approval of what seems most important to him: baseball.

ANSWER KEY

1. E	6. J
2. A	7. G
3. F	8. D
4. C	9. I
5. B	10. H

Name: _____

Date: _____

A Cap for Steve

Choose the correct word or phrase from Column B to complete each statement in Column A. Then put the corresponding letter in the space provided.

Column A

_____ 1. Steve Diamond is crazy about _____ .

_____ 2. By a wonderful stroke of luck, he becomes the owner of _____ .

_____ 3. Steve has an ally in _____ who understands his dreams.

_____ 4. The boy whom Steve caught with his property claimed that he _____ it.

_____ 5. Someone had _____ it from Steve's pocket.

_____ 6. Steve's father finally told him that he _____ their night in the ball park.

_____ 7. The lawyer's cold-hearted statement of how a policeman would settle the case made Steve's father protest that that would not be _____ .

_____ 8. In the encounter between _____ and his father, Steve thinks his father came out poorly.

_____ 9. Steve's father promises to _____ .

_____ 10. When they go into the fine apartment house, both Steve and his father feel _____ .

Column B

A. Eddie Condon's cap

B. stolen

C. bought

D. Mr. Hudson

E. baseball

F. his mother

G. justice

H. uncomfortable and out of place

I. help Steve train

J. enjoyed

A Christmas Memory

Truman Capote   Moderate

<u>SYNOPSIS</u>

Buddy, a boy at the time of the story, remembers Christmas preparations with his "friend," an elderly cousin with a child's delight in simple things. They live with stern, disapproving relatives, but he and she live for each other. In November, they begin gathering ingredients for their fruitcake-making ritual—no mean feat since they have very little money. The whiskey for the cake is the gift of Mr. Ha Ha, a fierce-looking saloon keeper, and the $12.73 they have earned over the year buys the rest. Their Christmas decorations are all homemade too, but the joy is in making them. Finally, the two are separated forever, but he treasures his Christmas memory.

<u>SUGGESTION</u>

In this tender Christmas story, Capote's skillful description makes the scene come alive. One device he uses often is the simile. Ask the students to find in the story similes—comparisons with *like* or *as*—that appeal to them. For example: "nickels and dimes worn smooth as creek pebbles" and "the black stove . . . glows like a lighted pumpkin."

ANSWER KEY

1. F	11. E
2. D	12. A
3. F	13. G
4. B	14. D
5. A	15. A
6. D	16. C
7. A	17. A, D
8. H	18. F
9. B	19. D
10. B	20. A

Name: _____

Date: _____

A Christmas Memory

Through this sensitively written short story, we share Buddy's (Capote's) Christmas memory. Let's see how many details made an impression on you. Match each description in Column A with the person or thing it describes in Column B.

Column A

_____ 1. Has survived distemper and two rattlesnake bites

_____ 2. "Is still a child"

_____ 3. A tough little orange-and-white rat terrier

_____ 4. A "giant with razor scars across his cheek"

_____ 5. Reminds his friend of a boy she knew in the 1880's

_____ 6. Has a face "not unlike Lincoln's, craggy . . . tinted by sun and wind"

_____ 7. Wants to be a tap dancer in the movies

_____ 8. Has colored lights that cast crazy patterns

_____ 9. Is gloomy and never laughs

_____ 10. Wants a fruit cake as pay

_____ 11. Talk about ruination, scandal, humiliation

_____ 12. Is sent to a military school

_____ 13. Serves to carry flowers, groceries, picnics, and firewood

_____ 14. Can tame hummingbirds

_____ 15. Imagines a "lost pair of kites hurrying heavenward"

_____ 16. Is iodine-dark and has bleached hair

_____ 17. Have a lovely kitchen party

_____ 18. Is kicked by a horse

_____ 19. Gradually fades away

_____ 20. Knows intuitively when his friend dies

Column B

A. Buddy

B. Mr. Ha Ha

C. Mrs. Ha Ha

D. Buddy's cousin

E. The relatives

F. Queenie

G. The buggy

H. Ha Ha's cafe

150 Great Short Stories

Christmas Morning

Frank O'Connor   *Easy*

SYNOPSIS

The narrator, Larry, dislikes his younger brother, Sonny, who acts superior and curries their mother's favor by showing off his spelling ability. Mother frequently praises Sonny to Larry and suggests that unless Larry mends his ways and studies, he will amount to nothing. Then, to make matters worse, Larry and his friend, Peter Doherty, skip school. When Mother finds out, she is very angry.

Smug Sonny tells Larry that Santa will punish him by bringing him no gifts. Although Larry scoffs, he is secretly afraid that Sonny is right. He decides to intercept Santa on Christmas Eve and explain why he skipped school, hoping that in person he can win Santa over.

On Christmas Eve, the parents have an argument over money, and Father leaves the house angrily. At bedtime, when the boys hang their stockings, he has not returned. Larry, trying to stay awake for Santa, hears his father come in about eleven, then falls asleep. At dawn, he wakes and checks the stockings, only to discover that Santa has left him a book, and Sonny, a popgun. He swaps the gun for the book from his own stocking, figuring that no one will know the difference. But Mother does, of course, and her anger at his deception is more than he can bear; suddenly he knows there is no Santa, only Mother, trying with too little money to give them a Christmas, and fearing that like his father, he will turn out to be "mean and common and a drunkard."

SUGGESTION

This story, by Ireland's master storyteller, effectively illustrates point of view. O'Connor lets us look at the world through the eyes of a young boy, full of bravado but secretly afraid that in his mother's eyes, he doesn't quite measure up to his brother.

ANSWER KEY

1. spell
2. skips
3. lied
4. leave him anything
5. talk
6. money
7. Father come in
8. book, pen and pencil, bag of sweets, pop gun
9. popgun, book
10. Mother

lang: skip school; bobbies: police; tuppeny: two pennies; quays: waterside paved areas for unloading cargo; publicans: bar owners

Reading Quiz:

Remembering the Details

Name: _____

Date: _____

Christmas Morning

In this exercise, you are asked to fill in the blanks with the appropriate word or words.

_____   1. Sonny's way of getting into his mother's good graces is by showing how well he can _____ .

_____   2. Larry, the narrator, gets into trouble when he _____ school with his friend, Peter Doherty.

_____   3. Mother is angry with Larry after the "langing" episode because he _____ . (past tense)

_____   _____   4. Sonny taunts Larry and tells him that Santa won't _____ .

_____   5. Larry decides to stay awake on Christmas Eve so that he can _____ to Santa.

_____   6. On Christmas Eve, Father and Mother argue over _____ .

_____   7. Just before eleven that night, Larry hears _____ .

_____   8. Early Christmas morning, Larry finds a _____ , a _____ , and a _____ in his stocking, but in Sonny's, he finds a _____ .

_____   9. Larry swaps the _____ and the _____ , figuring that no one will know the difference.

_____   10. That day, Larry finds out that there is no Santa Claus, there is only _____ , who is disappointed in him.

(continued)

Christmas Morning (continued)

Some Detective Work for You:

Look over the story again and try to decide from the context what each of these words, in common use in Ireland, means. Then write a definition in the space provided.

lang _____ (slang)

bobbies _____ (slang)

tuppenny _____

quays _____

publicans _____

A Story

Dylan Thomas *Moderate*

SYNOPSIS

The setting is Wales. The narrator is a young boy living with a very large uncle and a very small aunt. His uncle and several other men are planning a day's outing to Portcawl (which they never reach). Their pooled funds cover the cost of the bus, plus 20 cases of pale ale and a pound for each man to spend. When the boy's aunt carries out her threat to go home to her mother, he becomes part of the outing, although most of the day he sits outside pubs waiting for the others. Their outing includes a dip in a stream and sausages and mash cooked out in a field under the moon. Then the boy falls asleep.

SUGGESTION

Because Dylan Thomas's choice of words is so evocative, a worthwhile exercise would be to have the students review the story, listing similes, metaphors and adjective choices that they particularly enjoyed. For example: the uncle "breathing like a brass band," and the mouse-like aunt who "whisked about on padded paws."

ANSWER KEY

1. the uncle's waistcoat
2. the uncle's hair
3. the uncle's shoes
4. the men's best suits
5. the uncle and the boy in their Sunday clothes
6. the Mountain Sheep, a pub
7. the landlord
8. color of the men's faces after drinking
9. the uncle
10. the aunt

Open-Book Quiz:

Hunting for Word Treasures

Name: _____

Date: _____

A Story

As you know, Dylan Thomas was a poet who painted unusual pictures with words. Listed below are ten descriptive phrases from "A Story." Your job is to decide who or what is being described. Some of these phrases you may remember; others you must find in the text.

_____ 1. "A gravy-scented mountain"

_____ 2. A "forest fire" which "crackled among the hooked hams"

_____ 3. "Great black boots"

_____ 4. "Stiff and moth-balled and black"

_____ 5. "Cat-licked and brushed"

_____ 6. A place with a "thatched roof like a wig with ringworm"

_____ 7. "Long, lean, black-fanged"

_____ 8. "Beetroot, rhubarb, and puce"

_____ 9. "Big and trumpeting and red-hairy"

_____ 10. "Whisked about on padded paws"

The Day the World Almost Came to an End

Pearl Crayton   *Easy*

SYNOPSIS

It is 1936. The twelve-year-old narrator lives on a plantation with her church-going parents. On a Friday afternoon, she is playing in the watermelon patch when her cousin Rena comes running up, bursting with the news that the world is to come to an end on Saturday. The narrator looks to her father for reassurance, but still goes to bed remembering the minister's vivid description of Hell and recalling her own sins. A distant rumbling confirms her worst fears, and she runs out in her nightgown to warn the neighbors, but meets her father returning from church. When he tells her she has just heard an airplane, her world is miraculously restored.

SUGGESTION

In this short story, the narrator is recalling a childhood experience that had a profound effect on her. In preparation for a class discussion or for writing a theme, you might ask students to recall a memorable incident from their childhood that changed them in some way.

ANSWER KEY

1. Louisiana
2. on a plantation
3. in the melon patch
4. the church
5. an eclipse
6. She'd seen a rattlesnake in that field.
7. a long plank hitched under the plow
8. an airplane
9. rural and quiet
10. along the road past the other plantation cabins

The Day the World Almost Came to an End

_____ 1. In what state did the story take place?

_____ 2. Where exactly is the narrator's house located?

_____ 3. Where was the narrator when she heard the news that the world was coming to an end?

_____ 4. In the place where the narrator lived, what was the "axis" around which social life revolved?

_____ 5. What natural phenomenon was to take place on Sunday?

_____ 6. Why doesn't the narrator go at once to the cornfield to talk to her father about the world's coming to an end?

_____ 7. On what did the narrator ride?

_____ 8. What was the cause of the rumbling that wasn't thunder?

_____ 9. What does the fact that the narrator didn't recognize that rumbling sound show you about the area where she lived?

_____ 10. Where exactly did the narrator run when she was attempting to arouse the neighbors and alert them to danger?

Another April

Jesse Stuart   *Easy*

SYNOPSIS

It is a sunny April day in the Kentucky mountains. The narrator, a young boy, watches as his mother helps his 91-year-old grandfather into outer clothing for his first walk of the season. Then, from the window, the boy and his mother follow the old man's progress: He lifts his face to the spring breeze, watches a butterfly's flight, plays with a bumblebee, and stops to pat the hogs. But his destination is the smokehouse. There, a terrapin, even more ancient than Grandpa, has also come out to enjoy the April sun. The boy hears the old man talk to the terrapin, call it "old friend," and even bid it good-bye before turning back to the house. The boy accepts as fact that his grandfather and the terrapin communicate.

SUGGESTION

This short story demonstrates the advantages and disadvantages of first-person narrative. For example, the story is believable because the narrator seems to be sharing with the reader an event from his own experience. On the other hand, the boy can only relate what he sees or is told—thus the device of having the mother think aloud about how strong her father used to be, or telling the boy the terrapin's history. In that way, the author can supply the details that give the story significance.

ANSWER KEY

1. tells him how to dress
2. Grandfather wants independence.
3. They get shorter.
4. 91
5. examines and enjoys everything in nature
6. Both are old.
7. lumberjack
8. cocoon, bumblebee, butterfly, wind, hogs, dogwood
9. He is 95 years old.
10. tender, loving, sad

Reading Quiz:

Two Old Friends Meet Again

Name: _____

Date: _____

Another April

Answer each of the following briefly; six words per answer should be your maximum.

_____ 1. In what way does the boy's mother treat her father as if he were a child?

_____ 2. Why doesn't his mother let the boy go out on this first spring walk with his grandfather?

_____ 3. On succeeding springs, what has the boy noticed about the length of Grandpa's walks?

_____ 4. How old is Grandpa?

_____ 5. In what way has Grandpa retained the curiosity and enthusiasm of a young person?

_____ 6. Why does Grandpa feel kinship with his friend the terrapin?

_____ 7. What kind of work had Grandpa done as a young man?

_____ 8. Besides his talk with the terrapin, what other evidence is there in the story that Grandpa is fond of all living things? Use one example; there are several.

_____ 9. Why has Grandpa's family allowed this particular terrapin the privilege of living in the tomato patch in summer and under the smokehouse in winter?

_____ 10. What one adjective would you use to describe Mom's feelings as she watches Grandpa on his walk?

Manuel's Secret

Nancy Howe De Pagán

Easy

SYNOPSIS

Manuel, his two brothers, his little sister, and his parents are happy in the tiny house that the father has built. Each day, Father works cutting sugarcane; but the work is seasonal and there is not enough money for the family's needs, so he decides to accept his brother Julio's offer to go to New York where a factory job awaits him. The family take only what they can carry with them, but each child is allowed one memento: for Carmencita, her doll; Luis, a whistle; and Ramon, a kite. Manuel thinks carefully about his selection, but it is only when the family is settled in New York and very lonely that he reveals his choice—a song his grandmother taught him, one they can all sing to remind them of everything they loved and left behind.

SUGGESTION

"Manuel's Secret" is a story about choices: Papite's, to go to New York; the children's, to select their favorite toy; and Manuel's, to take a memory. Ask the students what their choice would be under similar circumstances.

ANSWER KEY

1. Puerto Rico

2. sugar-cane cutter

3. needs steady work

4. seeing her brothers and sisters

5. the buildings, subways, snow

6. doesn't want to go

7. doll, kite, whistle

8. The weather might be too cold.

9. warmth, mangoes, song of the tree toad

10. song his grandmother taught him

Reading Quiz:
Remembering the Details

Name: _____

Date: _____

Manuel's Secret

Fill in the blanks with the fewest possible words.

1. _____ Where did Manuel's family live?

2. _____ What was the father's job?

3. _____ Why did he decide to go to New York?

4. _____ What does the mother look forward to in New York?

5. _____ What are Manuel's brothers and sister eager to see in New York?

6. _____ How did Manuel feel about leaving his island home?

7. _____ What do Manuel's brothers and sisters take to New York?

8. _____ Why does Manuel decide not to take a *cequi* (tree toad) with him to New York?

9. _____ What three things do Manuel's brothers and sister miss when homesickness sets in?

10. _____ What was Manuel's choice to take with him to New York?

Night Game

William Melvin Kelley   *Moderate*

SYNOPSIS

In the opening paragraphs, the narrator shows that his is a loving family. He doesn't like the Saturday night poker parties though, because the next day his father sleeps late and doesn't take him to the park. He senses that the parties cause tension between his parents. One night he creeps out of bed to watch the game and realizes that his father is losing and is cross with his mother. The father is suspicious of one of the other players, and the boy's uncle tries to make peace. When the father loses, the boy, who had made a comment on one of the cards, is afraid that is what made his father lose. This makes him sad; but more important, for the first time he has felt fear of grown-ups and their anger.

SUGGESTION

In creating the setting, Kelley makes effective use of detail: "the sun . . . as big as a saucer and the color of orange sherbet"; "a star, netted like a snared white rabbit, in the tree outside my window." Ask the students to find five examples of such figurative language (metaphor and simile) in the story. To check how closely they read, ask how many of those phrases they noticed in their first reading.

ANSWER KEY

1. B	8. K
2. E	9. I
3. C	10. H
4. D	11. L
5. A	12. G
6. F	13. N
7. J	14. M

Reading Quiz:

An Unpleasant Awakening

Name: _____

Date: _____

Night Game

    In this short story, a child who has found the world a very happy place has an unpleasant awakening to a world of anger and frustration. Filling in the blanks in Column A with the right selection from Column B will give you an outline of the story and a review of what actually happened.

Column A

_____ 1. Saturday nights were times for _____ .

_____ 2. Saturdays were times to _____ .

_____ 3. Father's questioning Mother about the preparations for the party somehow caused the family to eat the rest of the meal _____ .

_____ 4. The boy woke up to hear _____ .

_____ 5. The boy crept out of bed to _____ .

_____ 6. He soon realizes that his mother is _____ and his father is _____ .

_____ 7. It is his father who says that the boy _____ .

_____ 8. The father claims a misdeal because the cards _____ .

_____ 9. The father wins a hand from _____ .

_____ 10. He calls his father's attention to _____ .

_____ 11. Afterwards, he thinks he made his father _____ .

_____ 12. The father challenges, saying he now knows why Bixby didn't _____ .

(continued)

Name: _____

Date: _____

Night Game (continued)

_____ 13. When his mother takes him to his room, the boy is crying, not because his father lost money, but because now, for the first time, _____ .

_____ 14. When the story ends, Mother has gone to bed, the guests have left, and the boy knows his father is _____ .

Column B

A. watch the card game

B. the weekly poker parties

C. in silence

D. low grumblings of joking men

E. run and play like an Indian

F. sleepy, annoyed

G. want to redeal

H. a card turned up on the table

I. the boy's aunt

J. might as well stay and watch

K. were not cut

L. lose the hand to Mr. Bixby

M. sitting alone in the kitchen

N. he was afraid of grownups

Sled

Thomas E. Adams   *Easy*

<u>SYNOPSIS</u>

At his mother's urging, a boy reluctantly apologizes to his sister for calling her a liar. Only then can he take his beautiful new sled out into the early-evening darkness. On his second run, he miscalculates, turns the sled over, bumps his head, and breaks a runner. Disconsolately, he fits together the jagged edges and starts home. Then he sees his sister come out of the house and cross the street to the grocery store. When she is on her way back, he offers to let her take a ride, knowing she could hurt herself. When she falls and apologizes, thinking she broke the runner, he tries vainly to explain.

<u>SUGGESTION</u>

In "Sled," the description appeal to the senses of sight, sound, and touch particularly, for example, "the steel runners shone blue in the light," and "the air silent and cold." To make students more aware of sense appeal as a writing device, ask them to find other examples in the story.

ANSWER KEY

1. No.

2. so that his mother will let him out

3. to put on his hat and be home by 7 o'clock

4. They are enemies.

5. He miscalculates and hits a snowbank.

6. surprise, disbelief

7. guilty; wants to stop her

8. apologetic; thinks she broke his sled

9. She won't listen.

10. She is kind and reminds him to put on his hat. He sees her in a new way and feels protective.

Name: _____

Date: _____

Sled

Answer each question briefly.

1. Is the boy's apology sincere? _____

2. Why does he apologize? _____

3. What are his mother's final orders? _____

4. What seems to be his relationship with his sister? _____

5. How is the sled's runner broken? _____

6. What is his sister's reaction when he offers to let her use his sled? _____

   _____

7. How does he feel when she starts out for the run? _____

8. What is her reaction after her fall? _____

9. Why doesn't he explain? _____

10. How does their relationship change? (Use two brief sentences.)

    _____

    _____

UNIT 11

OUTSIDERS

Stories of People Who Don't Fit In

UNIT 11

OUTSIDERS

Stories of People Who Don't Fit In **237**

Strangers in Town

Shirley Jackson

Moderate

SYNOPSIS

Addie Spinner, the narrator, begins by saying "I don't gossip," and then spews out gossip, suspicions, and fabrications that would do credit to somene much more imaginative. Although various neighbors are the subject of her barbs, she concentrates on the Wests, a young couple whom she refers to as "the crazy people." They moved in next door to her with their maid Mollie and her talking cat. In no way did they conform to the village mores. For that matter, they were probably unaware that they were misfits until a vigilante committee of mothers marched on their house and cruelly suggested that they move out of town; of course, they did.

SUGGESTION

In this short story, Jackson presents a caricature—deliberate exaggeration for effect. Her object, of course, is to show how suspicious people can be of anyone who is different and how vicious they can be in rejecting "outsiders." Ask the students to write a single sentence expressing the main idea (theme) which the story illustrates.

ANSWER KEY

1. D
2. E
3. A, B, E
4. F
5. E
6. A, B, E
7. G
8. C
9. H
10. B
11. Answers will vary.

Name: _____

Date: _____

Strangers in Town

You are asked to match the descriptions in Column A with the characters in
Column B. Finally, question 11 calls for you to express an opinion based on the story.

Column A

1. _____ She "doesn't gossip."

2. _____ She has a cat that apparently is fond of chicken.

3. _____ They are new in town. (3 answers)

4. _____ Her family wasn't noted for "keeping their senses right up to the end."

5. _____ She found the Acton child in the woods.

6. _____ They were all vegetarians. (3 answers)

7. _____ The grocer

8. _____ The doctor's wife and president of the garden club

9. _____ Apt to drive without a license

10. _____ Apparently works in the city

11. What significant point do you think Shirley Jackson makes in this story?

_____

_____

Column B

A. Mrs. West	C. Mrs. Acton	E. Mollie	G. Mr. Honeywell
B. Mr. West	D. Addie Spinner	F. Jane Dollar	H. Young Harris

Hands

Sherwood Anderson   *Moderate*

SYNOPSIS

Wing Biddlebaum had lived for twenty years just outside the town of Winesburg, Ohio, first with an aunt, and after her death, alone. But he was not a part of Winesburg, this recluse who talked freely with no one but George Willard, reporter for the *Winesburg Eagle*. George was aware that when Wing talked, his hands moved constantly, almost of their own volition, punctuating every word. He was curious, but he respected the old man too much to question him. Long ago, Biddlebaum had been a gifted teacher who inspired and loved the boys in his charge, but a cruel lie and suspicious people had broken his spirit and left him fearful of his fellow man.

SUGGESTION

"Hands" was one of Sherwood Anderson's most moving and compassionate stories and demonstrated all too clearly "man's inhumanity to man." Students need to know that the author was in revolt against the easy optimism of some of his contemporaries and wrote about American society with savage realism. In this story he shows that a man as gentle and good and intelligent as Adolph Myers (Wing Biddlebaum) could be destroyed by lies and ignorance and suspicion.

ANSWER KEY

1. understand
2. George Willard
3. hands
4. pick 140 quarts of strawberries
5. imitate others

6. Adolph Myers
7. teaching
8. lynched
9. his aunt lived there
10. human beings

Name: _____

Date: _____

Hands

Complete each question with the fewest possible words.

_____   1. People made fun of Wing Biddle-baum in Winesburg because he was different and they did not _____ him.

_____   2. His only friend was _____ .

_____   3. Wing Biddlebaum needed his _____ to talk.

_____   4. Wing's only claim to fame in Winesburg was the fact that he was able in one day to _____ .

_____   5. Wing advised George Willard that he would destroy himself if he tried to _____ .

_____   6. Wing Biddlebaum's real name was _____ .

_____   7. His profession was _____ .

_____   8. Because of lies and suspicion, Wing Biddlebaum came close to being _____ .

_____   9. He settled in Winesburg because _____ .

_____   10. The author says that for Wing Biddlebaum, the young reporter is the medium through which he expresses his love of _____ .

A Clean, Well-Lighted Place

Ernest Hemingway   *Moderate*

SYNOPSIS

In this famous short story, two waiters are in a Spanish cafe late at night with only one customer, an elderly deaf man who comes regularly. The waiters talk of the man's recent attempt at suicide, which the younger cannot understand because the man has money. The older waiter senses the customer's loneliness, his desire to remain in a "clean, well-lighted place," but the younger knows only that the man is keeping him from going home to his wife, and he treats him rudely, finally refusing to serve him more brandy. After closing the cafe, the older waiter goes to a bar himself for coffee, musing that all is *nada*.

SUGGESTION

This short story can be used effectively to demonstrate Hemingway's writing style—the short sentences, minimum of description, and use of dialogue to develop character. For example, we know the young waiter from what he says, his confidence and brashness, and his certainty that sex and money are the important things in life. A worthwhile writing assignment might be to ask the students to produce a brief dialogue imitating Hemingway's style.

ANSWER KEY

1. C	8. A
2. B	9. A
3. A	10. A
4. A	11. B
5. B	12. A
6. B	13. A
7. C	14. C

Name: _____

Date: _____

A Clean, Well-Lighted Place

Correctly matching the descriptions in Column A with the characters in Column B will demonstrate your understanding of this famous short story.

Column A

1. _____ Was well-to-do, old, and lonely

2. _____ Went to a bar himself after closing the cafe

3. _____ Wanted to go home to his wife

4. _____ Couldn't understand why anyone who had money would attempt suicide

5. _____ Understood a lonely person's need for "a clean, well-lighted place"

6. _____ Knew it was all *nada y pues nada* (nothing and for nothing)

7. _____ Lived with his niece, but was really alone

8. _____ Spoke rudely to the old man because he knew the man was deaf

9. _____ Because he was eager to close the cafe, refused the customer another brandy

10. _____ Said: "An old man is a nasty thing."

11. _____ Said: "I am of those who like to stay late at the cafe."

12. _____ Considered an hour more important to him than to his customer

13. _____ Lacked compassion and understanding

14. _____ Carried himself with dignity even though he'd had too much to drink

Column B

A. The young waiter   B. The old waiter   C. The customer

A Start in Life

Ruth Suckow

Easy

SYNOPSIS

A widow, Mrs. Switzer, lives with her three children in a shabby little house on the edge of town. Her earnings as a cleaning woman scarcely feed her family; this summer, the eldest girl, Daisy, must go to work as a mother's helper for the Kruse family, prosperous farmers. Daisy looks forward to her new status even though her mother tries to warn her that it won't be "like going visiting." Young Mrs. Kruse expects Daisy to keep busy, is indifferent to her complaints of "toothache," and has no intention of treating her like one of the family. Left alone when the Kruses go out for a ride, homesick Daisy weeps silently, for no one will comfort her.

SUGGESTION

Students will have little difficulty with the plot of "A Start in Life," and some will be able to identify with Daisy, away from home for the first time and faced with the indifference of strangers. But they may need help in seeing how effectively Suckow uses setting in this story, especially her description of the old, rundown, cluttered Switzer house in contrast to the shiny, bare, cold house which is home to the Kruses.

ANSWER KEY

1. Daisy
2. Mrs. Switzer's face
3. Elmer Kruse
4. the Switzer house
5. the Kruse house
6. Switzer bedroom
7. Daisy's bedroom at the Kruses'
8. Billy Kruse
9. Kruse kitchen
10. Edna Kruse

Name: _____

Date: _____

A Start in Life

In "A Start in Life" Ruth Suckow describes people and places very effectively. How much impression did those descriptions make on you? To find out, read the descriptive phrases, 1-10. Then see if you can supply the name of the person, place, or thing described.

1. _____ "Skinny, with pale sharp eyes set close together and thin, stringy reddish hair"

2. _____ A face "thin, weak, loving . . . drawn with neglected weeping, with its reddened eyes and poor teeth"

3. _____ An "old felt hat crammed down carelessly on his head, the back of his neck with the golden hair on the sunburned skin . . . strong and easy and slouched a little over the steering wheel"

4. _____ "Weathered to a dim color . . . the narrow sloping front porch whose edge had a soaked, gnawed look"

5. _____ "Small, modern, painted a bright new white and yellow"

6. _____ "Dark brown quilt and rumpled sheet . . . the door of the closet open, showing a confusion of clothes and shabby shoes"

7. _____ "A small old-fashioned bed, left from some old furnishings, that had been put in this room that had the pipes and the hot-water tank"

8. _____ "Fat, blond, in funny dark-blue union-alls"

9. _____ "Shining blue and white linoleum, the range with its nickel and enamel, the bright new woodwork"

10. _____ Her "young, fresh capable mouth was tightly closed"

The Fastest Runner on Sixty-first Street

James T. Farrell   *Easy*

SYNOPSIS

It is Chicago, 1919. Morty, a fourteen-year-old celebrity for his prowess at skating and running, is planning to enter high school in the fall and win more laurels, all for the sake of Edna Purcell, his dream girl. Morty's friend Tony is clumsy, stupid, and slow, but very strong. It is for Morty's sake that the boys begin to accept Tony. Later, Tony, who has had his share of racial slurs in the past, incites the other boys to gang up on a black. Morty, leading the pack as always, soon outdistances the others and follows the black boy into an alley. When Morty's friends catch up, they find only his "bleeding limp body."

SUGGESTION

This powerful story by James T. Farrell could be used as the basis for a discussion of the cruelty and tragedy that prejudice engenders. Students should note too that the story, which seems to be contemporary, was actually set in 1919.

ANSWER KEY

1. skating, running

2. to be the world's greatest runner

3. too slow

4. catching, beat up

5. beating up

6. racial slurs

7. four blacks had jumped him

8. Tony

9. Edna and how well he was running

10. he'd been thinking only of running and had forgotten his quarry

11. prejudice

Name: _____

Date: _____

The Fastest Runner on Sixty-first Street

Complete the following statements in the fewest possible words.

_____ 1. The two athletic skills that made Morty
proud of himself were _____ and
_____ .

_____ 2. Morty's dream was _____ .

_____ 3. The other boys teased Tony mercilessly
because he was _____ to catch them.

_____ 4. Morty helped Tony by _____ any boy
who teased or annoyed him; then Tony
would _____ the boy.

_____ 5. The only way Tony could gain approval
from the other boys was by _____
strange boys.

_____ 6. Tony's resentment of "colored boys"
came partly from his own ignorance and
partly from the _____ he had taken
from the other boys before he became
part of the gang.

_____ 7. Tony claimed the reason he lost his job
was that _____ while he was delivering
flowers.

_____ 8. The person who told Morty's gang
about the race riots was _____ .

_____ 8. Leading the mob of boys chasing the
two blacks from the park, Morty was
thinking only of _____ .

_____ 10. When the blacks jumped out of yards
and caught Morty, he was surprised. Why?

_____ 11. Who or what was really Morty's killer?

Defender of the Faith

Philip Roth

Moderate

SYNOPSIS

During World War II, Sergeant Nathan Marx is rotated back to the United States in charge of a company in basic training at Camp Crowder, Missouri. His first night, he meets recruit Sheldon Grossbart, who assumes that since Marx is Jewish he will be sympathetic to his requests which are endless. Grossbart is a master of manipulation who uses everyone to get what he wants, including assignment to Fort Monmouth, New Jersey, when everyone else is being sent to the Pacific. Marx outwits him on that one, though, and feels guilty that he has stooped to tactics worthy of Grossbart.

SUGGESTION

The title of the story, "Defender of the Faith," is ironic. Students should be aware that in irony what seems to be spoken in praise is actually blame. Was Grossbart actually a defender of the faith? Of course not; he used it—as he used everything else—to his own advantage.

ANSWER KEY

1. He uses it to get special treatment during basic training, especially from others of Jewish background.

2. No; he was unconcerned that they were being sent to Pacific as long as he didn't have to go.

3. Answers will vary. (Yes; he persuades others to manipulate records.)

4. He knew that Marx, being Jewish, would appreciate the importance of the Passover dinner; he knew Marx was softhearted.

5. Answers will vary.

Reading Quiz:

Thinking It Over

Name: _____

Date: _____

Defender of the Faith

Answer each of the following in one well-worded sentence.

1. In what way is Sheldon Grossbart's Jewish heritage useful to him?

   _____

   _____

2. Is he really concerned for the welfare of his buddies, Fishbein and Halpern? Explain.

   _____

   _____

3. In your opinion, is what Grossbart does unethical? Explain.

   _____

   _____

4. Why do you suppose Grossbart was pretty certain he could wangle a leave for himself and his buddies to go to "his aunt's"?

   _____

   _____

5. Sergeant Marx says: "Long ago, someone had taught Grossbart the sad rule that only lies can get the truth." What is your understanding of that statement, and do you agree with it?

   _____

   _____

What We Don't Know Hurts Us

Mark Schorer   Moderate

SYNOPSIS

A job transfer has forced Charles Dudley and his family to move to California. They are living in a house that doesn't suit them; it is surrounded by overgrown shubbery at which he hacks angrily in his spare time. His wife tries to make the best of things, but Charles, homesick for the East, feels "pinned down by a mortgage." When his nine-year-old son gets into trouble at school after "finding" a dollar in the coatroom, Charles bullies him, antagonizing the boy and his mother. At the end of the story, Charles realizes his mistake and is going out into the garden to find the boy and try to make amends.

SUGGESTION

If the students understand this short story, they will be aware that Charles is an outsider in two senses: first, as an unsuccessfully transplanted Easterner; and second, as a man out of touch with his wife and son. In a class discussion, students can decide if he is truly a victim of circumstance (the job transfer) or if his problems are self-made.

ANSWER KEY

1. B		6. B	
2. B		7. A	
3. A		8. B	
4. D		9. D	
5. D		10. C	

What We Don't Know Hurts Us

Below are listed the main characters in the story:

    A. Charles Dudley

    B. Josephine, his wife

    C. Penelope, their six-year-old daughter

    D. Gordon, their nine-year-old son

Your job in this exercise is to decide which of the characters is speaking in each of the quotations below.

1. _____ "I sometimes think that your disinclination to own anything is a form of irresponsibility."

2. _____ "I heard on the radio that Boston has had eighteen inches of snow."

3. _____ "Are you trying to make me homesick?"

4. _____ "Nobody likes me."

5. _____ "You hate me and I hate you." (This was written.)

6. _____ "We're all a nuisance that you're saddled with! We all just bother you."

7. _____ "Let's skip the psychology for a change. There is an old-fashioned principle of honesty and dishonesty."

8. _____ "I think Gordon's giving that dollar to that dreadful boy is one of the most touching things I've ever heard of."

9. _____ "He's my friend."

10. _____ "Why did Gordon steal money?"

Santa Claus Is a White Man

John Henrik Clarke   *Easy*

SYNOPSIS

Randolph Johnson, a little black boy, is on his way to buy Christmas presents for all his family with the 25¢ his mother gave him. Just after he passes a bedraggled white Santa, he meets a gang of white boys. They surround him and begin to taunt him as a crowd gathers to watch the fun. When Santa Claus takes over and begins to quiz him, Randolph is terribly frightened. Amid cries of "let's lynch him," the redheaded leader of the white boys goes to find a rope and bring it back. But Santa has apparently decided Randolph is too little to be worth lynching. Instead, he takes Randolph's quarter and gives it to the redhead. Seeing a chance to escape, Randolph runs off. His mother may give him another quarter, but even she won't be able to explain that terrible Santa Claus.

SUGGESTION

Because the story has some ambiguity (just why did Santa decide that Randolph should not be lynched?), students could offer their own opinion of Santa's motivation. For clues, they will want to reread the paragraphs that describe his change of attitude.

ANSWER KEY

1. 25¢
2. 4
3. his mother
4. poor whites
5. They might accuse him of stealing.
6. Randolph thinks he must be one of Santa's helpers.
7. a redhead
8. They are amused.

9. Santa Claus
10. to get a rope to lynch Randolph
11. "Niggers ain't got no business with money when white folks is starving."
12. Santa
13. gives him Randolph's quarter
14. throws a stone after him

Name: _____

Date: _____

Santa Claus Is a White Man

Fill in the blanks, using the fewest possible words.

1. _____ How much money does Randolph have for his Christmas shopping?

2. _____ How many gifts does he plan to buy?

3. _____ Who will receive the most expensive gift?

4. _____ To reach the business district, what kind of neighborhood must he pass through?

5. _____ Why is he afraid there?

6. _____ What is his reaction to the Santa Claus he sees?

7. _____ Who is the leader of the gang of boys?

8. _____ What is the reaction of the white adults when the gang members taunt Randolph?

9. _____ Who joins the crowd, takes control of the situation, and begins to quiz Randolph?

10. _____ What is the errand the redheaded boy undertakes?

11. _____ How does the man justify taking Randolph's quarter from him?

12. _____ Who makes the decision not to lynch Randolph?

13. _____ How does Santa "reward" the redhead?

14. _____ What does the redhead do when Randolph is running away from the crowd?

The Wise and the Weak

Philip Aponte   *Easy*

SYNOPSIS

Phil's family has moved to a new neighborhood on New York's Lower East Side. When he tries to makes friends, the other boys ignore him. After a fight with Ron, that "tough guy" invites Phil to join a club—a gang, really—whose initiation rite is to force Phil to cross Tarzan-like on an iron pipe laid between the rooftops of two buildings. The gang members then go off, leaving Phil dangling four stories above the alley. Eventually, cut and bruised, he gains his own roof. The next day, he tells his mother about it, but won't let her contact the police. Instead, they move back to the old neighborhood.

SUGGESTION

Since the narrator in this story simply reports what happened, making no attempt to figure out why it happened, there is a good basis for a lively discussion. Some questions students might try to answer are: Did Ron try to "get even" because Phil bested him in the fight? Would the gang have treated any outsider the same way? If so, why? Were they simply hoodlums seeking a thrill as they watched Phil struggle?

ANSWER KEY

1. basically unhappy and dissatisified
2. unfriendly, bullying
3. clever, sly
4. cruel, ruthless
5. weak, too eager to be part of the group

Name: _____

Date: _____

The Wise and the Weak

In "The Wise and the Weak," Aponte leaves it up to you, the reader, to decide what the characters are like and why they behave as they do. Some clues are in what they say. What does each of the following speeches reveal about the speaker?

1. Phil, the narrator, says: "I had just moved from the Lower West to the Lower East Side. Not much of a change! They were both dumps."

   _____

   _____

2. Ron's reaction when Phil grabs his arm and asks him why he is walking away: "Better watch that, Son, or next time I might get rough with you."

   _____

   _____

3. Ron's "reassurance" when Phil hesitates about proving himself to the gang: "Don't worry, Phil, it has nothing to do with defying the law."

   _____

   _____

4. Ron's "You'll never make it, Phil [when Phil contemplated making a run for the door to the stairs]. If you try and we catch you, we might—ah—accidentally on purpose throw you over."

   _____

   _____

5. Phil's " 'Look, Ron, what now, please? Please let me go.' A few tears slid down my face. I wasn't one of them. I guess I had known it from the beginning."

   _____

   _____

Effie Whittlesy

George Ade   *Easy*

SYNOPSIS

When her husband comes home, Mrs. Wallace tells him that she has hired a new and very efficient serving girl, one who seems almost too good to be true. When the girl comes into the dining room, she and Mr. Wallace are surprised to find they know each other; in fact, they were friends in the small town where they grew up. Mrs. Wallace decides she can't have a servant calling her husband Ed; Effie must go, and Mr. Wallace must send her. He does, in a very diplomatic way, but invites her to come back for a visit. Mrs. Wallace must be contented with that.

SUGGESTION

"Effie Whittlesy" is written almost entirely in dialogue, with little description, yet the reader learns a good deal about the characters. You might point out to the students that although effective dialogue is not easy to write, it is a clever way of characterization. To illustrate, ask the students to write a dialogue which tells the listener or reader what kind of people the speakers are.

ANSWER KEY

1. Mrs. Wallace; condescending
2. Mr. Wallace; cynical
3. Effie; loyal
4. Effie; high-principled
5. Mrs. Wallace; formal
6. Mrs. Wallace; snobbish
7. Mr. Wallace; practical
8. Effie; considerate
9. Mr. Wallace; tactful
10. Mrs. Wallace; snobbish

Reading Quiz:

Did You Listen Closely?

Name: _____

Date: _____

Effie Whittlesy

Identify the speaker in each of the following quotations and choose one adjective—for example, *friendly, suspicious, snobbish*—to indicate what attitude the speaker reveals.

1. _____ "She's from the country—and *green*! But she's a good soul, I'm sure."

2. _____ "Oh, she sings, does she? I knew there'd be some drawback."

3. _____ "I s'pose you know Mort has a position with the street-car company. He's doin' *so* well. I didn't want to be no burden on him, so I started out on my own hook . . . "

4. _____ "I'd about as soon handle a toad as a bottle of beer."

5. _____ "That will be all for the present, Effie."

6. _____ "Effie! Effie! And she called you Ed!"

7. _____ "I'll admit my past does not exactly qualify me for the Four Hundred, but it will be great if I ever get into politics."

8. _____ "But what'll your wife do? She told me today she'd had an awful time gettin' any help."

9. _____ " . . . I wouldn't like to see my wife giving orders to an old friend, as you are."

10. _____ "The idea! Did you invite her, really?"

UNIT 12

OTHER TIMES, OTHER WORLDS ═══

Fantastic Stories That Make You Ask "Could It Really Happen?"

UNIT 12

OTHER TIMES, OTHER WORLDS

All Summer in a Day

Ray Bradbury   Moderate

SYNOPSIS

The setting is a schoolroom on Venus filled with the children of the rocket men and women who had come to establish a civilization nine years ago. It has been raining for seven years, and now the sun is expected for two hours. Not one of the children, except Margot, has seen the sun. She is an outsider, having been on Venus only five years. There is talk that her parents may send her back to Earth next year. Before the sun comes out, the others lock Margot in a closet. Then, under a sun the color of "flaming bronze," they romp through a jungle the color of rubber and ashes, white cheese and ink. When the rain returns, they let Margot out.

SUGGESTION

To make the students aware of the effective use of color in this story, ask them to review details of Margot's appearance and the descriptions of the sun and the jungle. They should see how apt Bradbury's comparisons are—for example, a jungle the color of "white cheese"—and how they contribute to the mood of the story.

ANSWER KEY

1. on Venus

2. children of rocket men and women

3. rain

4. the sun

5. has seen the sun; has only been on Venus five years

6. They treat her as an outsider.

7. lock her in a closet so she misses the sun

8. 2 hours

9. Nothing is green.

10. Answers will vary.

Reading Quiz:

Taking Another Look

Name: _____

Date: _____

All Summer in a Day

Answer each question in the fewest possible words.

1. _____ Where does the story take place?

2. _____ Who are the principal characters?

3. _____ What has continued for seven years?

4. _____ What are the children eagerly anticipating?

5. _____ How is Margot different from the other children?

6. _____ What is their reaction to her?

7. _____ What do they do to her?

8. _____ How long does the sun stay out?

9. _____ What is missing in the jungle as the author describes it?

10. _____ What was your first reaction upon reading the story?

The Strawberry Window

Ray Bradbury *Easy*

SYNOPSIS

Bob and Carrie Prentiss and their children are living in a quonset hut on Mars. Carrie longs for her home on Earth and all its familiar things. Rockets come from Earth four times weekly. Bob remembers the front door, whose window contained a pane of strawberry glass. To please his wife, Bob uses most of his money to bring up in the freight rocket parts of their old house, including the strawberry window and his wife's piano. That much of their past they can keep, but they must push on to new frontiers, for the continuation of the race depends on what they can accomplish in their lifetime.

SUGGESTION

The theme of this fantasy is in Bob's conviction that when the sun blows up and Earth is no more, they must be safe on another planet. So that the race cannot be destroyed, mankind must spread out and seed the universe. In other words, we must break with the past and dare to cross new frontiers for survival's sake. Ask the students to find the main idea (theme) expressed in the story. Then ask them what that theme suggests to them.

ANSWER KEY

1. Mars

2. Bob and Carrie Prentiss

3. her house on Earth

4. the strawberry window

5. brings from Earth parts of their house and some furniture

6. Answers will vary.

7. believes the sun will explode and destroy Earth

8. People must spread out over the universe for survival.

The Strawberry Window

Answer the following questions in the fewest possible words.

1. _____ Where does the story take place?

2. _____ What are the names of the main characters?

3. _____ In her new life, what does the wife miss?

4. _____ What does the husband remember wistfully?

5. _____ To surprise his wife, what does he do?

6. _____ What do you remember of the description of Mars? Be brief!

7. _____ Why does the husband believe they must stay on this or another planet, not Earth?

8. _____ What does he see as their duty?

The Fairy Goose

Liam O'Flaherty   *Easy*

SYNOPSIS

An old Irish woman, Mary Wiggins, puts three goose eggs under her setting hen, but hatches only one gosling, a tiny creature unlike other geese in appearance and behavior. Mary and the other women decide the goose is a good fairy, and soon the other villagers are paying Mary money for spells and charms and treating the gentle little goose with great kindness. Finally, the priest hears of the people's superstitious behavior and denounces Mary while her neighbors watch. They turn from her and, claiming the goose is an evil spirit, stone it to death. From that time on, peace and harmony are lost from the village.

SUGGESTION

"The Fairy Goose" can be used to illustrate a literary genre, the fable—a short tale which contains a moral and often has an animal as its central character. Through discusssion, the students may arrive at the conclusion that the goose, who represented goodness, gentleness, and trust, was destroyed by superstition, suspicion, and greed.

ANSWER KEY

1. her husband
2. They thought it was a fairy goose.
3. is indifferent to them
4. earns her a profitable reputation for supernatural power
5. She is jealous; before the coming of the goose, she was believed to have magical powers.
6. It is frightened.
7. They think it is an evil spirit.
8. burning down Mary Wiggins's house
9. stoned to death
10. People become quarrelsome drunkards.

Name: _____

Date: _____

The Fairy Goose

Answer each of the following in one carefully worded sentence.

1. Who saves the "scraggy" little gosling's life when the old woman, out of pity, was going to kill it?

   _____

   _____

2. The author says the people of the village "paid more respect" to the little goose than they did to each other. Why?

   _____

   _____

3. How does the goose react to other geese?

   _____

   _____

4. How does the goose benefit its owner?

   _____

   _____

5. Why does an old woman choose to tell the priest about Mary Wiggins and her fairy goose?

   _____

   _____

6. When the priest speaks to the goose, how does it react?

   _____

   _____

(continued)

The Fairy Goose (continued)

7. How do the onlookers interpret the goose's behavior to the priest?

   _____

   _____

8. After the priest leaves, having told the people to "fear God and love your neighbors," what do they consider doing?

   _____

   _____

9. What is the poor goose's fate?

   _____

   _____

10. After Mary Wiggins cursed the village, what happened?

    _____

    _____

The Return of the Griffins

A.E. Shandeling   *Difficult*

SYNOPSIS

Gunar Vries, emissary to the U.N. from an unnamed European democracy, is alone in his hotel room late one night when a griffin appears from under the bed. Vries, once a professor of ancient Greek, recognizes his visitor and asks it politely why it has returned. The griffin explains patiently the enigma the world faces, with Vries and his kind working daily to promote the flowering of humanity while at the same time the prospect of atomic destruction is on everyone's mind. Vries writes to his president about his strange nocturnal visitor, saying the griffins will remain until the world decides its fate. As a result of the letter, he is recalled from his post and taken into protective custody. Vries travels away from Earth on the back of a griffin.

SUGGESTION

It is essential that the students reread and understand the griffin's explanation of why his kind is returning: "The U.N., a conference called to promote the flowering of humanity, and all the time the delegates hard put to it to breathe with the possibility of atomic dust in the air no more than five years from now . . . " Make certain they understand the meaning of *enigma*—in this context, something that is puzzling and contradictory. Then the griffin's comments will make sense to them.

ANSWER KEY

A. fabled monster: head and wings of eagle, body of lion

B. god of prophecy

C. Athenian statesman and orator

D. American statesman and orator

E. monster: head of woman, body of lion, wings of eagle

1. It is a puzzle to figure out why it has come.

2. was the god of prophecy

3. both orators and statesmen

4. She too posed riddles or enigmas.

Name: _____

Date: _____

The Return of the Griffins

Because this is a very unusual short story, you may find it difficult to understand unless you recognize the historical and mythological allusions (references) in it. Use a dictionary or other reference book to find a description or definition of each of the following. Then answer the four questions.

A. Griffin _____

B. Apollo _____

C. Demosthenes _____

D. Patrick Henry _____

E. Sphinx _____

And, of course, if you are not certain of the meaning of *enigma*, you should look it up too.

Now answer each of the following in the fewest possible words.

1. Why is the griffin's presence in itself an enigma?

   _____

   _____

2. Why is the reference to Apollo appropriate?

   _____

   _____

3. What did Patrick Henry and Demosthenes have in common?

   _____

   _____

4. Why do you suppose the griffin mentioned the Sphinx as being one of his kind?

   _____

   _____

Sam Small's Tyke

Eric Knight   Moderate

SYNOPSIS

Sam Small, a Yorkshireman, is left alone when wife Mully goes to America to visit their daughter. Although he spends his days doing chores and evenings in the pub, he is very lonely until he finds a small dog on the moors. He names her Flurry and soon finds that she is very intelligent, but he decides not to tell his cronies that she can talk! Flurry wins some contests of skill, and Sam wins a considerable sum in wagers. But then the rumor goes around that Sam has a young woman in his house. Indeed, Flurry can change herself into a girl at will, and someone has overheard her talking. Mully comes home, expecting the worst, but in the end, all is well.

SUGGESTION

"Sam Small's Tyke" is a tongue-in-cheek fantasy, of course, intended merely to amuse the reader. Students who have read some science fiction, also a kind of fantasy, should be able to pinpoint the difference between it and this short story. In science fiction, the author seems to be presenting reality, whereas Knight gets himself "off the hook" at the end of this story by saying: "Even Sam himself wonders at times if it can be true."

ANSWER KEY

1. B	6. E
2. D	7. I
3. J	8. G
4. F	9. A
5. H	10. C

Name: _____

Date: _____

Sam Small's Tyke

To test how well you remember this short story, match the descriptions in Column A with the characters in Column B.

Column A

1. _____ Sam Small's tyke

2. _____ The person who may have been the tyke's former owner

3. _____ The owner of the linen-drapery shop

4. _____ A betting man

5. _____ The tyke's competitor

6. _____ The biggest, strongest lad in all Yorkshire

7. _____ The sheep dealer who heard the tyke's voice

8. _____ The owner of the tyke's competitor

9. _____ A lonely man inclined to talk to himself

10. _____ Went to America to visit daughter Vinnie

Column B

A. Sam Small

B. Flurry

C. Mully

D. the gypsy man

E. Cawper

F. Gaffer Sitherthwick

G. Pettigill

H. Black Tad

I. Mr. Watcliffe

J. Miss Yeoby

Po' Sandy

Charles W. Chesnutt   *Easy*

SYNOPSIS

When the narrator's Northern wife decides she wants a backyard kitchen Southern style, he plans to salvage some lumber from a dilapidated one-room schoolhouse on his property. Knowing they will need more boards, he and his wife make a trip to the sawmill with their black coachman, Uncle Julius. The whine of the saw reminds Julius of the story of Po' Sandy, a slave so skillful that his master often lent him out for special jobs. Sandy's second wife, a "conjure" woman, turned him into a tree so that he could stay home, but Sandy was cut down and made into boards, eventually used for the "hanted" schoolhouse. The Northern wife loses interest in its lumber immediately. Uncle Julius and his friends are free to use it for their church!

SUGGESTION

Chesnutt, one of the earliest black writers (this story dates to 1899), was skillful in reproducing the dialect of his people. The students should be aware that a successful writer of dialect must solve several problems. First of all, he must have a good ear for dialect and reproduce its sounds faithfully. That, of course, involves problems of spelling. Then he must avoid in any way seeming to patronize the dialect-user; he must be sensitive and sympathetic. Last, he always runs the risk that a reader may not understand the dialect and may be "turned off." Through discussion, let the students give their reactions to the dialect in this story. Did they like it? Find it humorous?

ANSWER KEY

1. Civil War

2. She is a Northern woman, disapproving of slavery in general.

3. had swapped his wife for another black woman; paid Sandy a dollar

4. It was for a good cause.

5. Woodpeckers and turpentine gatherers attacked him.

6. She thinks it is a haunted place.

7. He wanted to use the schoolhouse as a church.

Name: _____

Date: _____

Po' Sandy

Answer each of the following in the fewest possible words.

1. The narrator says the schoolhouse has not been used since the "breaking out of the war." To what war does he probably refer?

   _____

   _____

2. Why is Uncle Julius certain that the narrator's wife will be interested in his story and sympathetic to Po' Sandy?

   _____

   _____

3. What unconsciously cruel thing had Sandy's master done in his absence? How did he compensate Sandy?

   _____

   _____

4. Tenie, Sandy's second wife, gave up conjuring when she "got religion." Why then was she willing to turn Sandy into a tree?

   _____

   _____

5. What were some of the tribulations Sandy had to contend with before he was taken to the sawmill?

   _____

   _____

6. What discourages the narrator's wife from wanting to use lumber from the schoolhouse?

   _____

   _____

7. What was Uncle Julius's real purpose in telling the story?

   _____

   _____

By the Waters of Babylon

Stephen Vincent Benét   *Moderate*

SYNOPSIS

The narrator, one of the Hill People and son of a priest, is training to become a priest himself. When he reaches maturity, he spends a night in the house of priesthood and undergoes purification. Then he sets out on his solitary journey to the forbidden Place of the Gods, an eight-day journey which entails building a raft to cross the great river. From legends, he knows of the great burning that took place there. He sees the ruins, but he also has a vision of it as it was before it was destroyed. He realizes it was a place of men, not gods, and returns home to tell his father of the truth he has discovered.

SUGGESTION

This short story will illustrate for the students how an effective title can help them to see the significance of a story. Babylon, in ancient times the richest and most magnificent of cities, is being compared with New York City, which, in the short story, had already reached its zenith and been destroyed.

ANSWER KEY

1. A. Subtreasury
    B. Washington
    C. Grand Central Station
    D. New York City

2. probably fire

3. They didn't stop to think of the consequences of what they were doing—their ceaseless building, their making tools for peace and war.

4. What men accomplished once, they can accomplish again.

Reading Quiz:

Some Puzzles to Solve

Name: _____

Date: _____

By the Waters of Babylon

Your answers to the following will demonstrate your understanding of this short story.

1. When he visits the Place of the Gods, John sees many ruins and finds fragments of lettering, including those in A, B, and C below. *D* he called the Place of the Gods. Identify any two.

   A. *UBTREAS* carved in stone near a "great heap of broken stones and columns":

   _____

   B. The statue of a man or god "with his hair tied back like a woman's"; his name on a cracked half of a stone was ASHING:

   _____

   C. The mighty temple with great caves and tunnels:

   _____

   D. Our name for the city he visited:

   _____

2. How had the Place of the Gods been destroyed? (Remember that this story was written in 1937.)

   _____

   _____

3. Explain briefly what you think John meant when he said: "Perhaps in the old days they ate knowledge too fast."

   _____

   _____

4. Why does John lose his fear when he realizes that the inhabitants of the great city had been men, not gods?

   _____

   _____

Silent Snow, Secret Snow

Conrad Aiken   *Easy to Moderate*

SYNOPSIS

Paul Haselman has found a secret world. Although each day he goes through the motions of dressing, answering his parents' questions, and sitting in the classroom, he is retreating more and more to the new place where snow muffles sound and shuts everything else out. It all began one morning while he was still in bed, waiting to hear the postman's footsteps as he came around the corner, but he never did! At least, Paul couldn't hear him until he reached the first house. Now, each day, the postman's footsteps begin one house closer to Paul's. Finally, the snow muffles them all the way, and the end comes in peace, cold, and sleep.

SUGGESTION

The ending of "Silent Snow, Secret Snow" allows students some leeway in interpretation. Some may be certain that Paul dies; others, that he had some kind of nervous collapse; still others, that the whole story is a dream sequence. In any case, it can be the basis for a good class discussion and will have students rereading carefully to support whatever conclusion they draw.

ANSWER KEY

1. secret world, gives him a sense of protection and seclusion

2. one morning in bed, as he waited for the sound of the postman's footsteps

3. He is withdrawn, doesn't always hear what people say to him.

4. causes misunderstanding and conflict

5. yes, suspects something is worrying him

6. Answers will vary.

Name: _____

Date: _____

Silent Snow, Secret Snow

Answer each question in one carefully worded sentence.

1. Which is more important to Paul, his secret world or the outside world of home and school? Why?

   _____

   _____

2. When did he first become aware of the snow?

   _____

   _____

3. How does Paul's awareness of the "secret screen of new snow between himself and the world" affect his behavior?

   _____

   _____

4. How does it affect his relationship with his parents?

   _____

   _____

5. Does the doctor come close to discovering Paul's secret?

   _____

   _____

6. What do you think happens to Paul at the end of the story?

   _____

   _____

Adventures of an Imp

Józef Mackiewicz   *Moderate*

SYNOPSIS

This unusual fantasy is the story of a little imp, son of devils, whose first job is to live on Earth in the family of a young manufacturer of dried fruits and suggest evil deeds to the children. An older devil supervises the imp while an older angel is there to prevent his harming the well-mannered children. The little imp witnesses the older devil's unsuccessful attempt to break up the family by introducing a wench to seduce the husband. But the wife forgives, and they are reconciled. Meanwhile, the little imp envies the children and tries unsuccessfully to enter their world of illusion. Instead, he is "sacked," but he has been the cause of one suicide, his first victory.

SUGGESTION

In this short story, everything is reversed. In fact, the devils come and go through mirrors. Ask the students to skim the story again to find these humorous reversals. For example, the imp's father is not "stuck in the mud," but "in the tar," and when the Father Devil is disgusted with his wife, he says: "The angels must have given me such a housekeeper."

ANSWER KEY

1. to play with matches and steal

2. "point of view enclosed in a circle"

3. by truth at the end of eternity (Answers will vary.)

4. on Earth

5. causes a suicide

6. Answers will vary.

Open-Book Quiz:

Taking Another Look

Name: _____

Date: _____

Adventures of an Imp

Find the appropriate passages in the short story to answer these questions in the fewest possible words.

1. What kinds of things is the imp learning in school?

_____

_____

2. How does the Father Devil describe Heaven and Hell?

_____

_____

3. How does the Father Devil suggest that Heaven and Hell may eventually be ruined?

_____

_____

What is your understanding of that statement?

_____

_____

4. Little Nick wants to "break away" into the world of illusion. Where is that happy world?

_____

_____

5. What is Little Nick's first success in his professional life?

_____

_____

6. What is your opinion of the story?

_____

_____

The Bottle Imp

Robert Louis Stevenson   *Easy*

SYNOPSIS

Keawe ships on a vessel for San Francisco to see the world. There, for $50, a man sells him a bottle whose imp will do anything the owner asks. But the imp cannot prevent death, and its owner will go straight to hell. When Keawe tells the ship's mate, Lopaka, about the bottle, his advice is to make a wish. When Keawe returns to Hawaii, his wish for a beautiful house is granted. Lopaka buys the bottle (it must always be sold for less than the owner paid) and disappears. Keawe falls in love with Kokua, but discovers he has a terrible disease; he buys the bottle back for 1¢ to rid himself of the sickness. Cured, he marries Kokua, but the shadow of damnation hangs over him. Kokua tries to save him, and he tries to save her. Then a greedy boatswain makes off with the bottle, and they live on happily.

SUGGESTION

This short story is a variation on the old theme of a man who sells himself to the devil to gain material wealth. In this case, students should see that Keawe and Kokua's great selfless love for each others saves them. Some students may have read Benét's *The Devil and Daniel Webster*, which has similarities to this story.

ANSWER KEY

1. B	9. I
2. K	10. H
3. C	11. L
4. D	12. O
5. F	13. M
6. E	14. N
7. A	15. J
8. G	

Name: _____

Date: _____

The Bottle Imp

Fill in the blanks for the statements in Column A with the appropriate word or phrase from Column B.

Column A

_____ 1. Keawe ships aboard a vessel bound for San Francisco because he wants _____ .

_____ 2. Whoever dies owning the bottle faces _____ .

_____ 3. Keawe is admiring an _____ when he meets the owner of the bottle.

_____ 4. Keawe and Lopaka discover that the imp in the bottle is _____ .

_____ 5. When Keawe returns to Hawaii, he learns of the _____ .

_____ 6. The people of _____ avoid Keawe and Kokua because they fear the couple.

_____ 7. When Keawe is about to be married, he discovers he has the _____ .

_____ 8. When Keawe is sad, Kokua is sad too because she is afraid she _____ .

_____ 9. Keawe and Kokua are finally free of the bottle because of a _____ .

_____ 10. Kokua asks _____ to buy the bottle from Keawe on her behalf.

_____ 11. The rule of the bottle is that each owner must sell it for _____ he paid for it.

_____ 12. It is _____ that eventually saves Keawe and Kokua.

_____ 13. Lopaka's advice to Keawe is _____ .

_____ 14. When Keawe sells the bottle for $60, it _____ .

_____ 15. When Keawe buys the bottle for 1¢, Kokua cleverly suggests that it can be resold for _____ .

Column B

A. Chinese Evil

B. to see the world

C. unusually attractive house

D. evil-looking

E. Tahiti

F. death of his uncle and cousin

G. does not please him

H. an old man

I. greedy boatswain

J. centimes

K. damnation

L. less than

M. make a wish

N. returns

O. their love

UNIT 13

EXPLORING THE HIDDEN
WORLD OF THE MIND

Stories to Help You Understand Why People Behave As They Do

UNIT 13

EXPLORING THE HIDDEN WORLD OF THE MIND
Stories to Help You Understand Why People Behave As They Do 283

The Angel of the Bridge

John Cheever

Moderate

SYNOPSIS

At 78, the narrator's mother still skates in Rockefeller Center, but is afraid of flying. When his older brother confesses his fear of elevators, the narrator thinks the brother's delusion that the building might fall down is absurd. Then one day, as the narrator is crossing the George Washington Bridge in a thunderstorm, he has a panic attack, thinking the bridge is about to collapse. Suddenly, his whole world seems full of brutality and chaos. A second panic attack on a bridge demoralizes him further. Then, as he is about to cross a bridge once more, he picks up a young, cheerful, blond hitchhiker, carrying a cardboard suitcase and a small harp. She rides only to the other side of the bridge, but his crossing is peaceful.

SUGGESTION

"The Angel of the Bridge" contains a symbol already familiar to the students, the bridge—"Don't cross your bridges until you come to them," "He burned his bridges behind him," etc. Ask them what they think the bridges symbolize in this story and why they struck terror in the narrator's heart. A clue is his wish to go back to a simpler, more peaceful world.

ANSWER KEY

1. Answers will vary. (unseemly; not in the usual pattern)

2. sees it as absurd, shows no compassion, won't accept that he could be like that

3. breaking with the past, facing the future

4. superficial, based on his maintaining self-esteem, "saving face"

5. Answers will vary.

Name: _____

Date: _____

The Angel of the Bridge

Answer each of the following in a carefully worded sentence.

1. It seems to bother the narrator and cause him some annoyance that his elderly mother still skates. Why should that bother him?

   _____

   _____

2. What attitude does he take toward his brother's elevator phobia?

   _____

   _____

3. There are actual bridges in this story—the George Washington Bridge, the Tappan Zee Bridge. What do you think the bridges represent (symbolize) in the narrator's mind?

   _____

   _____

4. What clue do you have to the narrator's relationship with his wife?

   _____

   _____

5. What is your explanation of the hitchhiker, the angel of the bridge?

   _____

   _____

A Visit of Charity

Eudora Welty

Easy

SYNOPSIS

A fourteen-year-old Campfire Girl is about to visit someone in the Old Ladies' Home because it will earn her three points. When the nurse asks her if she knows any of the residents, she says: "Any of them will do." The nurse shoves her into a room with two old women and leaves. One tries to be friendly; the other is bitterly antisocial, resenting the forced intimacy of a roommate and now a visitor. As for the Campfire Girl, she wants only to escape. The sprightly one says it is the other's birthday. When the girl goes closer to the bed, she realizes the unfriendly old woman is crying. After the briefest of visits, she leaves, having done her duty.

SUGGESTION

This story delineates the tragedy of lack of communication between human beings. The girl has no empathy for the old women, and they have little for each other. Ask the students to put into a sentence the message they think Eudora Welty wants her readers to find in this story.

ANSWER KEY

1. perfunctory, impersonal (Answers will vary.)
2. to earn points in her Campfire program
3. Everything "smelled wet."
4. indifference
5. unenthusiastic
6. It is her birthday.
7. The woman is crying.
8. unsympathetic
9. money
10. retrieves her apple

A Visit of Charity

Answer each question as briefly as possible.

1. _____ What adjective would you use to describe the nurse's attitude?

2. _____ Why is the young girl visiting the Old Ladies' Home?

3. _____ What is the girl's reaction to the old ladies' room?

4. _____ What is indicated to you by the fact that the girl hadn't even looked at the potted plant she brought?

5. _____ When the friendly old woman says she and her roommate enjoyed the visit of the Campfire Girl who read the Bible to them, what is the other old lady's attitude?

6. _____ What is significant about the day for Addie, the old woman in the bed?

7. _____ When Marian looks closely at the woman in the bed, what does she notice?

8. _____ What is the other woman's attitude when Marian tells her that her roommate is crying?

9. _____ What does the friendly old woman ask for when she goes with Marian to the door?

10. _____ What is the first thing Marian does when she gets out of doors?

The Piece of String

Guy de Maupassant   *Easy*

SYNOPSIS

Among the Norman peasants bringing their animals and produce to Goderville on market day is M. Hauchecombe. A thrifty man, he stoops to pick up a piece of string on the road and is embarrassed to see his enemy, M. Malandain, watching. That day he is summoned to the mayor's office. A pocketbook containing money was lost, and Malandain claimed that the pocketbook was what Hauchecombe picked up. Hauchecombe is not arrested, and the man who found the pocketbook returns it to its owner, but Hauchecombe has retold and embroidered his story so much that people suspect he is hiding something. Obsessed with the incident, Hauchecombe sickens and dies.

SUGGESTION

De Maupassant is careful to establish that M. Hauchecombe, like the other peasants at the fair, is a "sharp dealer," suspicious of his fellow men. It is easy for his acquaintances to believe the worst of him because they are all capable of the thing he is accused of. It would be worthwhile to ask the students what moral the story points out. Perhaps they will conclude that we should show charity toward others.

ANSWER KEY

1. He is naturally thrifty.

2. They hate each other.

3. suspicious; trying to drive a hard bargain

4. astounded and terrified

5. He ignores it.

6. He is known for "sharp dealing."

7. The injustice of the suspicion breaks his heart.

Reading Quiz:
Thinking It Over

Name: _____

Date: _____

The Piece of String

Answer each question briefly.

1. _____ Why does M. Hauchecombe pick up the piece of string?

2. _____ What is his relationship with M. Malandain?

3. _____ How would you describe the general attitude of the peasants at the market?

4. _____ What is Hauchecombe's reaction when he is accused?

5. _____ When Hauchecombe gives his oath that he is telling the truth, what is the mayor's reaction?

6. _____ Why don't people believe Hauchecombe?

7. _____ What kills M. Hauchecombe?

The Chrysanthemums

John Steinbeck   *Moderate*

SYNOPSIS

A ranch wife, Elisa Allen, is setting out young chrysanthemums. Some distance away, her husband is discussing business with two strangers. Later, he tells her he has sold some steers for a good price and suggests that they go out that evening for dinner and a movie to celebrate. She continues her planting until a peddler comes along in a shabby wagon with a mismatched team and a mongrel dog. She find him strangely attractive, but he flatters her only because he wants to make a sale. She pots some chrysanthemums for him, and he seems pleased. Later, as she and her husband are driving to town, she sees the plants discarded on the road and feels rejected herself.

SUGGESTION

Students may have difficulty understanding Elisa Allen's actions. Certainly they will be aware that she finds the peddler attractive, but there are indications too that she chafes at a woman's role, thinks she can do many things as well as a man, and envies the peddler's independence. Ask the students to find passages that illustrate each of these attitudes.

ANSWER KEY

1. strong

2. She thinks she could do as well as a man.

3. praises her garden

4. to flatter Elisa

5. She thought they had much in common.

6. He's free and independent.

7. She wants to feel attractive.

8. that she looks strong and happy

9. She feels rejected.

Reading Quiz:

Understanding the Characters

Name: _____

Date: _____

The Chrysanthemums

Answer each question briefly. None will require more than ten words.

1. _____ What one adjective is used several times to describe Elisa (the first time in reference to her face)?

2. _____ Why is Elisa especially interested when her husband says, referring to the chrysanthemums, "I wish you'd work out in the orchard and raise some apples that big."

3. _____ What does the peddler say that persuades Elisa to find some work for him?

4. _____ Since the peddler threw the chrysanthemum shoots away, the woman with the nice garden whom he mentioned to Elisa probably didn't exist. Why did he make her up?

5. _____ Why did Elisa find the man attractive?

6. _____ Why does she envy his way of life?

7. _____ Why does she dress and make up so carefully?

8. _____ Henry tries to compliment Elisa on her appearance. What does he say?

9. _____ Why does Elisa cry at the end of the story?

Everything That Rises Must Converge

Flannery O'Connor   *Difficult*

SYNOPSIS

Julian lives with and is supported by his mother, a widow of good family and small means. He scarcely bothers to conceal his scorn for her; she is completely adoring of him, blind to his faults, and patient in the face of his rudeness. Her grandfather, she proudly recalls, had two hundred slaves. Now she must adapt to a world where their descendants are her equals.

Mother and son go together to her exercise class; because she is afraid to ride the "integrated" buses at night, Julian is an unwilling escort. When a black man boards the bus, Julian, hoping to irritate his mother, attempts unsuccessfully to draw him into conversation. But Julian notices his mother's flushed face and obvious discomfort and feels he has made his point.

A large, angry-looking black woman comes aboard with her little boy. The child clambers up beside Julian's mother while the woman settles beside him. His mother takes great delight in the child, oblivious to the black woman's angry attempts to retrieve him. When all four get off at the same stop, Julian attempts to discourage his mother from offering the child money, but she persists. The black woman, seething with resentment at the "condescension," knocks Julian's mother down and strides off. At first, Julian is too busy berating his mother to realize she has had a stroke. Then he does, and that is "his entry into the world of guilt and sorrow."

SUGGESTION

With advanced students, this story can be an effective basis for a discussion of individual perceptions of reality. How does Julian's world differ from his mother's? What is the black woman's view of the world? Whose is the "real" world?

ANSWER KEY

1. Since he scorns her, he refuses to admit his dependency on her.
2. His mother needs to maintain the social standing that she thinks is her birthright.
3. She is patient, loving, and self-sacrificing.
4. She is limiting how far they can rise in status, never to the point where they have equality with the whites.
5. He sees himself as superior to people like his mother. He seeks conversation with blacks only because he wants to show his tolerance, not because he truly wants to know them better.
6. She hates all whites and feels they condescend to her.

Name: _____

Date: _____

Everything That Rises Must Converge

Answer each of the following in one carefully worded sentence.

1. In the opening paragraph, describing Julian's relationship with his mother, Flannery O'Connor writes: "Julian did not like to consider all that she did for him." Why would he prefer not to consider his mother's sacrifices for him?

   _____

   _____

2. Julian thinks to himself: "Since this had been a fashionable neighborhood forty years ago, his mother persisted in thinking they did well to have an apartment in it." Why would his mother *need* to think that way?

   _____

   _____

3. What good qualities in his mother does Julian overlook?

   _____

   _____

4. Julian's mother says of the blacks' change in status: "They should rise, yes, but on their own side of the fence." What is obviously wrong with her statement?

   _____

   _____

5. Julian sees himself as "free of prejudice and unafraid to face facts." Give one instance that shows his own prejudice or his preference for fantasy over reality.

   _____

   _____

6. What is the black woman's prejudice and how is it expressed?

   _____

   _____

Sherrel

Whit Burnett

Moderate

SYNOPSIS

The narrator, now eighteen, talks about the year he was nine, the year his five-year-old brother Sherrel died of scarlet fever. He was always impatient with his brother and didn't want him tagging along, so Sherrel was left much to himself. One day, playing with the older kids, the narrator discovers that he can peel the skin off his hands. Sherrel wants to see this, but the narrator drives him away. The narrator had had scarlet fever without even knowing it and believes he "gave" it to Sherrel. He still carries a burden of guilt and is trying to make amends, perhaps by writing poetry and signing Sherrel's name: "I would be more him too, then."

SUGGESTION

Although the narrator is young, he has already known the finality of death and the guilt of not having been kind enough to someone while he was alive. Ask the students what can be learned from the narrator's experience.

ANSWER KEY

1. nine

2. eighteen

3. guilt

4. be bothered

5. five

6. scarlet fever

7. quiet, thoughtful

8. "Do you want your little sister to die too?"

9. artist-writer

10. Sherrel's name

Reading Quiz:
Recalling the Details

Name: _____

Date: _____

Sherrel

Complete each of the following statements in the fewest possible words.

1. _____ At the time of his brother's death, the narrator was _____ years old.

2. _____ At the time he tells the story, he is _____ .

3. _____ He still feels _____ when he thinks of his brother's death because he blames himself for it.

4. _____ The narrator failed his brother by not wanting to _____ with him.

5. _____ Sherrel was _____ years old when he died.

6. _____ The actual case of Sherrel's death was _____ .

7. _____ Sherrel was a (*two words*) boy.

8. _____ At one point, the narrator's mother added to his guilt by saying, in effect, _____ .

9. _____ The narrator wants to be an _____ .

10. _____ He considers writing poems and signing them with _____ .

You Should Have Seen the Mess

Muriel Spark   Moderate

SYNOPSIS

The narrator's preoccupation with cleanliness colors every judgment she makes. She didn't qualify for Grammar School, but preferred the Secondary Modern because it was "more hygienic." At seventeen, she took a typing job in a lawyer's office and found little to recommend it except that the glass in the bookcase was clean. She "kept in with" Dr. and Mrs. Darby in order to meet people, but complained about their children's shabby clothes and the chipped paint and "cracked lino" in their house. She liked Willy Morley, a well-to-do young artist, "in a way," but "his place was a terrible mess," and she was certain it would "break" her "heart to sink so low."

SUGGESTION

Students need to realize that "You Should Have Seen the Mess" is a caricature—an exaggeration for effect. The girl, totally lacking in humor, judges everyone by the shallowest of standards and finds no one who can measure up to her absurd expectations.

ANSWER KEY

1. humorous (Answers will vary.)

2. Answers will vary.

3. Answers will vary.

4. how clean they were

5. Because the narrator could not appreciate the charm of the 14th-century cottage, she didn't realize that anyone would live there by choice.

6. talented, kind, tolerant

You Should Have Seen the Mess

Answer the following questions briefly.

1. Use one adjective to describe your initial reaction to the story.

   _____

2. What do you think was the author's purpose in writing the story?

   _____

   _____

3. How did you like the narrator?

   _____

   _____

4. What was her only criterion for judging people?

   _____

   _____

5. Why did she think Dr. Darby's mother should apply for public housing?

   _____

   _____

6. What kind of person is Willy Morley?

   _____

   _____

The Sentimentality of William Tavener

Willa Cather   *Moderate*

SYNOPSIS

William Tavener is "the most prosperous farmer in McPherson County," but people credit much of his success to his wife, Hester, who continually drives her husband to more and more effort. Hester is as voluble as William is silent. In making certain that their sons get everything she thinks they deserve, she pits herself against her husband at times. In this story, her argument that the boys should be allowed time for the circus sets off a string of reminiscences between husband and wife and rekindles an intimacy they had long forgotten. When she defends her husband, the boys realize they have lost their ally.

SUGGESTION

This subtle characterization by Willa Cather will require careful reading. You might point out that Hester's single gesture of taking the mosquito net from her cherished wax fruit and placing it over William's face as he lies sleeping symbolizes a change in her attitude toward her husband and, incidentally, toward her sons.

ANSWER KEY

1. She gives him advice before he asks.

2. He admires her for it.

3. his wife's gowns and bonnets

4. He corrects her and says the circus she attended had a camel and a dromedary, not two camels.

5. Generally, they talk about money.

6. She thinks of her girlhood and her wedding.

7. that they have lost their ally against their father

The Sentimentality of William Tavener

Answer each of the following questions in one sentence.

1. Why doesn't William Tavener need to consult his wife about business matters?

   _____

   _____

2. What is William's attitude toward his wife's "gift of speech"?

   _____

   _____

3. When William goes over the bills, what are the only purchases to which he never objects?

   _____

   _____

4. What is Hester's first hint that William was frivolous enough to take time off for the circus when he was a boy?

   _____

   _____

5. Hester and William's conversation about their mutual recollections of the circus of their childhood soon becomes an exchange of other memories. How is that conversation different from their usual talks with each other?

   _____

   _____

6. After William gives her ten dollars for the boys' circus money and goes to bed, what memories crowd Hester's mind?

   _____

   _____

7. When she cautions her sons not to waste their father's hard-earned money, what do the boys realize?

   _____

   _____

The Witness

Katherine Anne Porter

Moderate

SYNOPSIS

Uncle Jimbilly, an old black handyman, fascinates the children with his ghost stories and makes them feel faintly guilty with tales of the horrors of slave times. He is willing to make intricately carved wooden tombstones for every small beast or bird the children want to bury, but is apt to become suddenly annoyed and make fierce threats "to skin somebody alive" or "pull out somebody's teeth." Of course, he never "gets around" to any of these things, but he keeps warning them that "everybody had better look out."

SUGGESTION

Uncle Jimbilly is intended as a parody of Uncle Remus, Joel Chandler Harris's kindly old storyteller. To help students understand the term *parody*, you might suggest that it is a literary caricature. Thus, Jimbilly is as fierce—dwelling on horror, violence, and death—as Remus is gentle. As a special assignment, one or two students might read Uncle Remus stories and report on them so that the class can make a comparison.

ANSWER KEY

1. handyman

2. carving miniature tombstones

3. talks about the days of slavery

4. He only did what he felt like doing.

5. No.

6. Answers will vary.

7. implies retaliation for what the slaves suffered (Answers will vary.)

Reading Quiz:

Understanding a Character

Name: _____

Date: _____

The Witness

Answer the following questions as briefly as possible.

1. _____ What is Uncle Jimbilly's work?

2. _____ What is his special talent?

3. _____ What does he do that both fascinates the children and makes them feel guilty?

4. _____ The author says the children thought Uncle Jimbilly had "got over his slavery very well." Why did they think that?

5. _____ By his own admission, was Uncle Jimbilly ever treated as a slave?

6. The author states that Uncle Jimbilly was "very religious," but in the next paragraph describes the horrible things he threatened to do. In your opinion, was he religious?

_____

_____

7. Why do you think Uncle Jimbilly threatened to "skin people alive" or "pull out their teeth"?

_____

_____

The Other Child

Olivia Davis

Moderate

SYNOPSIS

The main characters in this powerful story are the narrator, a frustrated and bitter woman whose husband left her long ago to raise their blind son alone, and that son, Lansing, now thirty-five. He is a sad young man, dependent on his mother, yet aware that she has little affection for him and that his physical dependency gives her a sense of power she enjoys.

Their rented summer cottage is so close to the beach that bathers are "sitting practically under the porch railings." From that vantage point, the mother watches a young woman who is alone except for her toddler. After a day or two, the girl attracts the attention of one of the lifeguards, as the narrator had anticipated sourly. The girl, Rose, recently divorced, and the lifeguard, Johnny, soon fall in love. Lansing finds their relationship touching, but his mother scoffs at it as a casual affair.

The climax comes on a wild, stormy day when the beach is deserted except for Rose and Johnny. They are too engrossed in each other to see her little boy wandering into the waves. Lansing, sensing danger, stumbles wildly onto the beach, but he, like the lovers, is too late to save the child. The mother merely watches.

SUGGESTION

This is an ideal story to illustrate the effective use of first-person narrative. The mother's character is so clearly revealed through her warped reactions to other people that no explanation of her behavior is needed.

ANSWER KEY

1–5: Any combination of M, R, T, F, S

6–10: Any combination of C, A, D, G, K

11–15: Any combination of P, Q, E, N, B

16–20: Any combination of O, J, H, I, L

Thinking it over: married late, child born blind, husband deserted her

303

Name: _____

Date: _____

The Other Child

In this exercise, you are given details about all four of the characters. Your task is to match the detail with the character.

CHARACTER:

The mother, Nettie (the narrator)

1. _____
2. _____
3. _____
4. _____
5. _____

The son, Lansing

6. _____
7. _____
8. _____
9. _____
10. _____

The girl, Rose

11. _____
12. _____
13. _____
14. _____
15. _____

The lifeguard, Johnny

16. _____
17. _____
18. _____
19. _____
20. _____

DETAILS

A. Had a heavy, pasty face

B. Had "true-blue" eyes

C. Was slow and awkward

D. Thought it would be wonderful to be "perfectly ordinary"

E. Had bleached hair with the roots showing

F. Was very bitter

G. Believed in young love

H. Had five brothers and sisters

I. Was friendly and sympathetic

J. Liked children and wanted some

K. Was melancholy

L. Began neglecting his job

M. Was deserted by her husband, Harold

N. Wrote long letters and tore them up

O. Was a college student, studying sociology

P. Wore a yellow bathing suit

Q. Was divorced less than two weeks

R. Claimed that she didn't snoop

S. Hadn't ever expected to marry

T. Had a cruel streak

THINKING IT OVER:

Explain briefly what events in the narrator's life helped to make her the kind of person she has become.

_____

_____

UNIT 14

ANOTHER POINT OF VIEW

Stories to Help You Look at the World in a New Way

UNIT 14

ANOTHER POINT OF VIEW
Stories to Help You Look at the World in a New Way 305

A Mother's Tale

James Agee   Moderate

SYNOPSIS

A cow, her calf, and the other spring calves watch a cattle drive in the distance. The calves want to know where the cattle are going. Somewhat reluctantly, the cow tells them about the railroad. Her own calf wants to go too, but she tries to convince him and the others that it is better to stay safely at home. Their questions about the final destination of the train goad her into telling them about one who took it and managed to come back, a grisly story of the slaughterhouse and his painful journey homeward to warn the others: "We are brought into this life only to be victims . . . unless we save ourselves. . . . Never be driven."

SUGGESTION

Point out to the students that "A Mother's Tale" is a *fable*. You may want to use this definition: "A short tale with a moral, often with an animal as its central character." In discussion, the students should decide this short story's significance. A clue would be the admonition, "Obey nobody. Depend on none. Each one is himself, not of the herd . . ."

ANSWER KEY

1. Near the edge. Following the crowd, people lose their individual identity.

2. They are not safe at all; they are going to be slaughtered.

3. They felt secure and happy.

4. He had a purpose, to warn the others.

5. Her calf is determined to go anyway. The littlest calf missed the point.

Name: _____

Date: _____

A Mother's Tale

Answer each question in one carefully worded sentence.

1. The fifth paragraph (which begins: "From the hillside . . . ") describes the moving mass which is the herd. Where is the only place that individual animals are discernible? In symbolic language, what do you think Agee is saying?

   _____

   _____

2. Reread the paragraph which tells about loading the train. What is ironic about the statement, "When everybody is safely in, they slide shut the doors"?

   _____

   _____

3. Reread the section in which the cow is retelling the legend of The One Who Came Back. What was the reaction of the cattle when they reached their destination and were given such good food and water?

   _____

   _____

4. Reread to discover how The One Who Came Back found the strength for the return journey. What was his source of strength?

   _____

   _____

5. In the closing lines of the story, what indication is there that the cow's retelling of the legend, painful as it was for her, hasn't served its purpose?

   _____

   _____

Sonny's Blues

James Baldwin   *Difficult*

SYNOPSIS

The narrator is teaching his algebra classes but thinking of the news item—his brother Sonny has been picked up for selling and using heroin. Out of touch with his brother, he gets the details from another addict who had been Sonny's friend. When his little daughter dies, he finally contacts Sonny, whose letter in return is both apologetic and sympathetic, and they are reunited when Sonny is again free. The narrator remembers their growing-up years—his mother's concern for Sonny, their conversation after her death when Sonny says he wants to be a jazz musician—but he never understand's Sonny torment or the power in his music until he goes to a club and hears "Sonny's Blues."

SUGGESTION

James Baldwin was an eloquent spokesman for his people. "Sonny's Blues" demonstrates the alienation, fear, and hopelessness that was part of the narrator's and Sonny's growing-up years in Harlem. Ask the students to find references in the story to all of these emotions. For example, the narrator's memory of twilight on Sunday afternoons: "When light fills the room, the child is filled with darkness. He knows that every time this happens, he's moved just a little closer to the darkness outside."

ANSWER KEY

1. the boys' father	6. Sonny
2. the boys' mother	7. Sonny
3. Sonny	8. the narrator
4. Sonny's friend	9. Sonny
5. Creole	10. the narrator

Name: _____

Date: _____

Sonny's Blues

Part of the problem between the brothers in "Sonny's Blues" is that they cannot communicate because the narrator doesn't really listen to Sonny. If you "listened" closely as you read, you will know which of the characters made each of the following significant statements.

1. _____ "Safe! Safe, hell! Ain't no place safe for kids, nor nobody."

2. _____ "Your daddy never did really get right again. Till the day he died, he weren't sure but that every white man he saw was the man that killed his brother."

3. _____ "I think people ought to do what they want to do. What else are they alive for?"

4. _____ "I ain't smart. If I was smart, I'd have reached for a pistol a long time ago."

5. _____ "You got a real musician in your family."

6. _____ "All that hatred and misery and love. It's a wonder it doesn't blow the avenue apart."

7. _____ "It struck me all of a sudden how much suffering she must have had to go through—to sing like that. It's repulsive to think you have to suffer that much."

8. _____ "You're getting to be a big boy. It's time you started thinking about your future."

9. _____ "I hear you. But you never hear anything I say."

10. _____ "I won't forget. I won't let nothing happen to Sonny."

Adam

Kurt Vonnegut, Jr.   *Easy*

<u>SYNOPSIS</u>

Two men are in a Chicago lying-in hospital waiting room. They are Sousa, already the father of six girls, and Knechtmann, small, hunched, weary-looking. When the nurse announces that Sousa's wife has yet another baby girl, he leaves in disgust, predicting sourly that Knechtmann will father a son. Knechtmann and his wife, refugees who "had grown up behind barbed wire," have already lost one child, and he dreams that this baby will carry on his family name. When his son is born, Knechtmann is delighted, but everyone who hears his news is indifferent. He feel deflated until he talks to his wife and shares her joy in their child, the symbol of their survival.

<u>SUGGESTION</u>

Students need to be aware that Vonnegut's allusion to Adam, the father of the race, is also a reference to Knechtmann, who sees the infant as the new beginning of a family which had been virtually destroyed. Thus, the title of the short story emphasizes its theme.

ANSWER KEY

1. He died a little as he watched each member of his family being led away to be killed by the Nazis.

2. No, he just hopes it will live; if it is a girl, it will be named for his mother.

3. Not really; he's tired and indifferent.

4. He has no one to call.

5. The others are really only interested in baseball.

6. Harry is polite, but Heinz senses that he and the girl are indifferent.

7. his wife's joy that they have survived and have their baby

Name: _____

Date: _____

Adam

Answer each of the following in one brief sentence.

1. Why does Heinz Knechtmann feel so much older than his twenty-two years?

   _____

   _____

2. Does Knechtmann really care whether the child to be born is a girl or a boy? Explain.

   _____

   _____

3. Does the doctor share Knechtmann's delight in the birth? Explain.

   _____

   _____

4. When Knechtmann reaches the bank of telephone booths, why doesn't he make a call to spread the good news?

   _____

   _____

5. After Knechtmann share his good news with Sousa and the bartender, why does he feel so alone?

   _____

   _____

6. When Knechtmann meets Harry, his co-worker, and Harry's girlfriend, he tells them his news. How do they react?

   _____

   _____

7. What restores Heinz's sense of awe at the miracle of birth?

   _____

   _____

The Almost White Boy

Willard Motley

Moderate

SYNOPSIS

Although Jim has white skin and blond hair, he is a mulatto whose white father and black mother are shunned by their neighbors. Finally, they move to a poorer area of mixed nationalities where they are no longer conspicuous. When Jim finishes school, he "passes as white" to get a job in a downtown hotel. When he meets Cora, he falls in love with her and tells her his secret. She seems to return his love, but she is reluctant to have him meet her parents and warns him not to tell them he is black. When she invites him to make love, he refuses, saying he wants to wait until they are married. She calls him a name and walks off.

SUGGESTION

"The Almost White Boy" demonstrates the effective use of irony in a short story. Jim's father's belief that "people are just people," a belief that Jim adopts, is disproved for Jim and his father. Both of them are "rejected" and made to feel "different." There is irony too in that Cora considers herself broad-minded, but she is actually as prejudiced as her parents. She is eager to have Jim make love to her, but insulted when he proposes marriage.

ANSWER KEY

1. B	9. H
2. C	10. D
3. J	11. E
4. G	12. F
5. I	13. B
6. A	14. D
7. G	15. G
8. A	

The Almost White Boy

In this story, the dialogue reveal each speaker's attitude clearly. In Column A are significant remarks made by each of the characters. Your job is to match each remark with one of the characters in Column B.

Column A

1. _____ "I want it to be right for us . . . Will you marry me?"

2. _____ "People are just people. Look—and remember."

3. _____ "There are plenty of fine upright Negroes—I'm sure. Of course I don't know any personally . . . "

4. _____ "Do you mean about you being colored? It doesn't matter to me . . . "

5. _____ Told stories about "Florida niggers"

6. _____ "You ain't no different. My ma says so. You're just a nigger!"

7. _____ "You damn dirty nigger"

8. _____ "You're a white nigger—white nigger."

9. _____ "Ah'm glad to meetcha . . . You sho' got good taste, Jim."

10. _____ "We can't go on the street together without everybody staring at us. You'd think we'd killed somebody."

11. _____ Thought Jimmy looked like "poor white trash"

12. _____ "Say, what are you anyway?"

13. _____ "I'm Polish."

14. _____ " . . . they say I had to marry out of my race— that my own color wasn't good enough for me."

15. _____ "I never liked Nig—Negroes. You're not like a Negro at all."

Column B

A. Lorenzo and Ruby

B. Jimmy

C. Jimmy's dad (Mr. Warner)

D. Jimmy's Mom

E. Aunt Beulah-May

F. Jimmy's friend Tony

G. Cora

H. Slick Harper

I. Cora's father

J. Cora's mother

The Fifty-Yard Dash

William Saroyan   *Easy*

SYNOPSIS

Twelve-year-old Aram answers an ad in *Argosy All-Story Magazine* and is deluged with letters from Lionel Strongfort, who promises a body-building course for a price. Aram finally persuades his Uncle Gyko to give him the $3.00 necessary to buy Strongfort's secrets of success. They turn out to be standard good-health practices combined with an exercise regimen which Aram follows only briefly. With no training but excessive self-confidence, he goes into a track meet, prepared to defeat all comers, with the inevitable result. He emerges sadder but, unfortunately, not wiser.

SUGGESTION

Students who are able to look beneath the surface in a piece of literature might try to find the irony in this short story. Uncle Gyko realizes Strongfort is a charlatan, promising gullible Aram a shortcut to success, yet Uncle Gyko is actually as self-deluding as his nephew. Gyko looks for his own shortcut to success, but lacks the pertinacity to reach his goals.

ANSWER KEY

1. D   6. B

2. I   7. G

3. A   8. A

4. J   9. E

5. C   10. F

Bonus: the grandmother

Name: _____

Date: _____

The Fifty-Yard Dash

Choose from Column B the word or words that correctly answer the questions in Column A. (Hint: One word or phrase is used twice.)

Column A

1. _____ What was Aram really looking for when he answered Lionel Strongfort's ad?

2. _____ After Strongfort's first letter, what did Aram decide to become?

3. _____ What kept Aram from answering Strongfort's letters?

4. _____ What did Strongfort's secrets consist of?

5. _____ What helped Aram's uncle release the "mysterious vital forces" within himself?

6. _____ In the uncle's opinion, where does his strength come from?

7. _____ What was Uncle Gyko's word to describe Lionel Strongfort?

8. _____ In Aram's opinion, what was the only obstacle to his obtaining the success Strongfort's letters promised?

9. _____ What was the actual reason for Aram's disappointing performance in the race?

10. _____ What quality do Aram and his uncle have in common?

Column B

A. lack of money

B. God

C. yoga

D. a shortcut to success

E. lack of self-discipline

F. self-deception

G. liar

H. a strong, well-developed body

I. the most powerful "man" in the area

J. sensible eating habits and exercise

Bonus question! (The answer does not appear in Column B; you must supply it.)

Who is the most practical member of Aram's family? _____

The Magic Carpet
Joseph Wechsberg
Moderate

SYNOPSIS

The setting is Prague, Czechoslovakia, during the Russian occupation after World War II. Kocian, an airport waiter, thinks wistfully of the past, before shortages and restrictions on travel virtually destroyed the restaurant's business. Kratochvil, cashier of the airport's branch bank, comes in for a hot drink. From his remarks, Kocian suspects that Kratochvil is dreaming about escaping on one of the American planes that make a scheduled stop there, a familiar dream to Kocian. Later, the self-important customs inspector, Pelc, comes in to say that Kratochvil is now in custody, suspected of stockpiling dollars for escape. Ironically, Pelc reveals that he too dreams of life in the United States.

SUGGESTION

Setting is important here. From Kocian's reveries about the past and the author's description of the present, students should be able to describe how war and Soviet control changed life for the three ordinary people in this short story.

ANSWER KEY

1. B	7. A
2. A	8. C
3. A	9. A
4. C	10. All want to escape to America.
5. C	
6. B	

Name: _____

Date: _____

The Magic Carpet

Although the three major characters in the story have one thing in common, their positions and their attitudes are quite different. Each of the descriptions or quotations in Column A fits only one of the characters in Column B. Your job is to match the character with the description or quotation.

Column A

1. _____ An educated man who spoke several languages

2. _____ As a boy, had dreamed of having a magic carpet

3. _____ Hated himself for laughing with Pelc

4. _____ Had built his own radio

5. _____ "I've been on to him for three months, but I wanted to be sure."

6. _____ Was a courier for the underground during the German occupation

7. _____ Had worked in New York for his brother-in-law

8. _____ "That _____ ! Always afraid somebody might slip through." (Who is being referred to?)

9. _____ Knew exactly where the coal was and couldn't do a thing about it except curse in the privacy of his mind

10. _____
    Finally, what do the three men have in common?

Column B

A. Kocian, the waiter

B. Kratochvil, the cashier

C. Pelc, the customs man

Editha

William Dean Howells

Moderate

SYNOPSIS

Editha, who finds the threat of war exciting, thinks her fiancé must make himself worthy of her by becoming a hero. But he is peace-loving and not at all certain that he wants to enlist. Editha decides to send back his letters and ring with a letter of her own: the man she marries "must love his country first of all." When George, her fiancé, enlists, she gives him her letter to read later. He is killed in the first skirmish. Editha, still playing a role, goes West to visit his mother, but is not received as she had expected to be. The mother accuses Editha of sending her son to war and says she is glad he died before he killed anyone else. But Editha still does not gain self-knowledge; in fact, she thinks the woman is deranged.

SUGGESTION

Students may find Howells' style difficult. He uses long sentences and paragraphs; his choice of words may not be in their vocabulary; and his subject—a condemnation of war, war fever, and the Spanish-American War in particular—is serious. It might help to analyze one or two of the longer paragraphs in class, finding the topic sentence and seeing how the author supports it. Students will gain understanding and may pick up a pointer or two from a man who was a master prose stylist.

ANSWER KEY

1. Caught up in war fever, she felt he should do something heroic to make himself worthy of her.

2. George's father lost an arm in the Civil War and came home with grave misgivings.

3. writes him a letter saying that the man she marries "must love his country first of all"; makes a packet of his letters and her engagement ring, but does not send it

4. It is when he comes back late at night to say he has enlisted.

5. It was partly Editha's attitude, partly that the men looked up to him, partly war fever.

6. She detests her, blames her for George's going to war, and threatens to tear off Editha's mourning clothes.

7. She may to some extent, for she did feel shame; but to "save face" she prefers to think the woman is deranged.

Name: _____

Date: _____

Editha

To demonstrate your understanding of the characters, answer each of the following questions in one carefully worded sentence.

1. Why was Editha so convinced that her fiancé should go to war?

   _____

   _____

2. What specifically in George's background has made him skeptical about war as a means of settling any dispute?

   _____

   _____

3. What does Editha do when she is still not certain that George will enlist?

   _____

   _____

4. When does she give her letter to George?

   _____

   _____

5. Why did George enlist?

   _____

   _____

6. What is George's mother's reaction to Editha?

   _____

   _____

7. Why doesn't Editha understand the woman's reaction?

   _____

   _____

The Key

Isaac Bashevis Singer   *Easy to Moderate*

SYNOPSIS

Since her husband's death twenty years ago, Bessie Popkins has retreated more and more from the world, leaving her apartment only when she has to, for she is certain that everyone is planning to rob her. On this afternoon, she goes to the supermarket. Indecisive, she spends two hours there and walks home at sunset only to break her key in the lock of her apartment door. Confused and friendless, she goes out again and spends the night in the doorway of a church where she does some soul-searching. After she returns to her apartment, she become aware too late of people's kindness, for that day she is again with Sam.

SUGGESTION

If the term *epiphany* is one your students are mature enough to know or understand, the experience Bessie has—"a new perception of reality by means of a sudden intuitive realization"—which makes her aware that people are interdependent and are worthy of love is, of course, an epiphany.

ANSWER KEY

1. evil; about to prey on her

2. She doesn't trust banks.

3. doesn't care anymore

4. all falling apart

5. She doesn't trust him.

6. She thinks he's up to some sly trick.

7. She begins to realize how selfish and indifferent she has been.

8. to start a new life, perhaps remarry

9. kindly

10. to join Sam

Reading Quiz:

Thinking It Over

Name: _____

Date: _____

The Key

Answer each question very briefly.

1. _____ In the years since her husband died, how has Bessie come to view her neighbors?

2. _____ Why does Bessie have money, stocks, and bonds hidden throughout the apartment?

3. _____ Why does she no longer keep track of her income and expenses?

4. _____ What is her opinion of New York? America? The world?

5. _____ When Bessie breaks her key in the lock, why doesn't she call the superintendent?

6. _____ What is Bessie's reaction to the man's politely holding the door for her?

7. _____ What happens to Bessie at the church?

8. _____ What decision does she make?

9. _____ When she returns, how do the superintendent and the neighbors treat her?

10. _____ Where does Bessie go at the end of the story?

Sex Education

Dorothy Canfield Fisher   *Moderate*

SYNOPSIS

The narrator was in her early teens when she first heard her Aunt Minnie tell "the story" intended then as a warning to young girls. Minnie, who as a sixteen-year-old had spent a summer in the Middle West, got lost in a field of tall corn and was attacked by the minister in whose house she was staying. Minnie was fifty-five when she told "the story" again. In this version, the minister was surprised by Minnie's throwing herself upon him in her relief to find someone familiar—an innocent encounter. By the final telling of "the story," Minnie, now in her eighties, is aware of what the minister's feelings must have been and pities him.

SUGGESTION

"Sex Education" gives us insights, not only about our attitudes toward sex, but also about our changing perceptions of reality. Since some students may have difficulty expressing themselves on the subject of sex in a classroom discussion, it might be more effective to ask each one to write in a brief essay why Aunt Minnie's story changed so much with each retelling.

ANSWER KEY

1. She had frightened Minnie, but had given her no real guidance.

2. in her sympathetic treatment of her son, and her retelling "the story" for the girls

3. She was ashamed to.

4. They thought in those days that if they didn't talk about something unpleasant, it would almost seem as if it had never happened.

5. She realizes he must have known his scarred face was revolting to her and would be to any woman of his own age.

6. Answers will vary.

Sex Education

Answer each question in one carefully worded sentence.

1. When Aunt Minnie, then in her fifties, recalled her cousin Ella's warnings about the cornfield, in what way did she think Ella had failed to make them effective?

   _____

   _____

2. What evidence do you have that Minnie herself, as a mature woman, tried to be more helpful to adolescents than her cousin had been?

   _____

   _____

3. According to Minnie's first version of "the story," why didn't she tell on the minister?

   _____

   _____

4. How does Minnie explain the fact that no one questioned her carefully about the man she claimed had "scared" her?

   _____

   _____

5. In her old age, when Minnie thinks about the minister in the cornfield, she feels compassion for him. Why?

   _____

   _____

6. In your opinion, which version of Minnie's story comes closest to the truth? Explain.

   _____

   _____

Night Club

Katharine Brush   *Easy*

SYNOPSIS

Mrs. Brady, attendant in the ladies' room of Club Français, regularly comes to work with a magazine or newspaper for her free moments—accounts of murder or divorces or the funnies are her favorites. Until the dance act goes on at one o'clock, she is busy as a maid to the young and not-so-young women who come in. She sees one remove her wedding ring as a prelude to an evening out. Another tells a friend of her husband's infidelity. One seems determined to "shake" her boyfriend waiting outside the door, while another is about to elope. Mrs. Brady, however, is interested only in her tips, and when her "break" comes, is immediately engrossed in her magazine's "true stories."

SUGGESTION

"Night Club" can be used to demonstrate irony in fiction. In this case, Brush puts Mrs. Brady in a setting where real-life drama takes place each night. It is ironic that Mrs. Brady, through ignorance or indifference, is oblivious to reality and seeks vicarious thrills by reading "true stories," the *semblance* of reality, to liven up her dull evening.

ANSWER KEY

1. read "real-life" stories in a magazine

2. bored, interested only in the money

3. elopement, "escape" from a boyfriend, talk of one husband's infidelity with two of his wife's friends

4. probably not—was a bit shabby, owner out to "take" the customers

Name: _____

Date: _____

Night Club

Answer each of the following questions briefly.

1. Mrs. Brady has the "best seat in the house" to observe real drama each night. What does she prefer to do instead?

   _____

   _____

   _____

2. How would you describe her attitude toward her job?

   _____

   _____

   _____

3. Name three exciting things that happened while she was on duty this Saturday night.

   _____

   _____

   _____

4. Do you think Club Français was a high-class establishment? Explain.

   _____

   _____

   _____

UNIT 15

THEY DARED TO STAND
UP AND BE COUNTED

Stories of People with Courage and Conviction

UNIT 15

THEY DARED TO STAND UP AND BE COUNTED

Stories of People with Courage and Conviction **327**

The Last Lesson

(also called "The Last Class")

Alphonse Daudet   *Moderate*

SYNOPSIS

Little Franz is late for school and expects a scolding, but when he arrives, the teacher, M. Hamel, tells him in a kind tone to be seated. Everything is different this day, Franz notices. M. Hamel wears his best clothes, the children are "strange and solemn," and the back benches are filled with adult villagers. Then the teacher announces that German, not French, is now to be the language in the schools of Alsace-Lorraine. He talks then of the importance of their native tongue and accuses himself and them of not being diligent enough in teaching and learning it. His final act is to write *Vive la France!* on the blackboard.

SUGGESTION

Ask the students when they think the incident in the story took place. Chances are they will assume it was during World War II and will be surprised to learn that Daudet died in 1897. His war was the Franco-Prussian War of the 1870's.

ANSWER KEY

1. news of lost battles, the draft, and orders from German commanding officers

2. He knows what Franz will hear, and that school will not be the same without the French language.

3. The teacher wears his best clothes, the children are very quiet, the adults sit in the back of the room.

4. He regrets that he didn't study more.

5. He regrets that the parents didn't urge their children to go to school and that he wasn't diligent enough in teaching the language.

6. Answers will vary.

7. He is moving after 40 years.

8. He writes *Vive la France!* on the blackboard.

The Last Lesson

Answer each of the following in one carefully worded sentence.

1. Franz, the narrator, is quite young, but old enough to have noticed that the town bulletin board in the past two years has had only bad news. What kinds of things have been posted?

   _____

   _____

2. Why does the blacksmith, having just read the notice on the bulletin board, tell Franz not to hurry, that he'll get to school in plenty of time?

   _____

   _____

3. What is different about the atmosphere of the schoolroom when Franz arrives?

   _____

   _____

4. What does Franz regret when he hears the news about his native language?

   _____

   _____

5. What does the teacher, M. Hamel, regret?

   _____

   _____

6. What do you think M. Hamel meant when he said: "When a people are enslaved, as long as they hold fast to their language, it is as if they had a key to their prison."

   _____

   _____

7. What personal reason does M. Hamel have for feeling sad?

   _____

   _____

8. What is his final act in the classroom?

   _____

   _____

A&P

John Updike

Easy

SYNOPSIS

The narrator is a nineteen-year-old checkout clerk in an A&P, bored with his job and the customers. Then three girls in brief bathing suits come in; one, whom he dubs "Queenie," leads the others confidently. He and the other checkout clerk are fascinated by the girls' appearance and their progress throught the store. When the manager sees the girls he tells them they must be "decently dressed" to shop in the A&P. They are embarrassed and leave as quickly as they came, but not before the narrator has told the manager, in protest, "I quit."

SUGGESTION

Students will probably see Sammy's gesture as a gallant defense of the girls, but they should also note passages in the story that show his attitude toward his other women customers. He is generally scornful, calling them "sheep" and describing one as a "witch."

ANSWER KEY

1. a witch

2. sheep

3. scornful

4. her voice, bearing, and what she buys

5. Answers will vary.

6. probably to let them know he's "on their side," but also to get credit for courage

7. doesn't give them credit for much intelligence

8. Answers will vary.

Name: _____

Date: _____

A&P

Answer the following questions in the fewest possible words.

1. _____ When Sammy, distracted by the girls, rings up a customer's purchase twice, and she protests, what does he call her?

2. _____ What word does Sammy use to describe the other customers pushing their carts through the store?

3. _____ Sammy says his partner's customer is "an old party in baggy grey pants." From that remark and others, what do you think is his usual attitude toward his customers?

4. _____ On what does Sammy base his judgment that "Queenie" is "tony"?

5. Do you think the manager was justified in speaking to the girls about their dress? Explain.

   _____

   _____

6. Why does Sammy want to be certain that the girls hear him say "I quit"?

   _____

   _____

7. Think over Sammy's comment: "You never know for sure how girls' minds work (do you really think it's a mind in there or just a little buzz like a bee in a glass jar?) . . . " What does it show about his attitude toward girls?

   _____

   _____

8. If the women in bathing suits had been older, do you think Sammy would have been "on their side"? Explain.

   _____

   _____

The Demonstrators

Eudora Welty   *Moderate to Difficult*

SYNOPSIS

Dr. Richard Strickland, like his father before him, ministers to all the sick and dying in his Mississippi town. On this night he cares for a young black maid, stabbed with an ice pick by her common-law husband, and then for the husband, whom she stabbed in return and who was left for dead by his fellow blacks. In the house where the young woman lies dying, none of her own people seem especially concerned, and the white newspaper account of the "mishap" is concerned only with pointing out that it had no racial significance. Strickland is weary and discouraged with the lack of compassion on both sides.

SUGGESTION

This short story opens and closes with a reference to Miss Marcia Pope, the ancient retired schoolteacher who scorns both medication and tranquilizers. The students should see her as a symbol of an orderly rational world, a disciplined world which no longer exists in Holden, if, indeed, it ever did.

ANSWER KEY

1. She refuses medication or tranquilizers, preferring to live in the orderly world of her mind.

2. curious, unemotional

3. Answers will vary.

4. by questioning the inaccurate newspaper account; in other words, questioning whether or not the end justified the means

5. that it had no racial significance

Name: _____

Date: _____

The Demonstrators

Answer each question as briefly as possible.

1. No doubt you have heard the expression "mind over matter." How does it apply to Miss Marcia Pope, the elderly bedridden schoolteacher who amuses herself by reciting literature she learned long ago?

_____

_____

2. How would you describe the attitude of the onlookers as the young black woman lies dying?

_____

_____

3. What is your understanding of the reason the doctor's wife separates from him after their handicapped daughter dies?

_____

_____

4. How had the doctor offended the student civil-rights worker?

_____

_____

5. What seemed to be the most important detail of the stabbing incident as far as the white newspaper was concerned?

_____

_____

The Land of Room Enough

E.P. Maxwell

Easy

SYNOPSIS

Fourteen-year-old Manuel, eldest of the seven children of a Puerto Rican couple recently transplanted to New York, has come with dreams of "the land of room enough" described in a poem. However, his family has to settle for one room of a four-room apartment which already houses three other families—twenty-two people in all. When Manuel discovers that the "landlord," Jesepo, is illegally subletting the apartment and taking advantage of his countrymen, the boy is determined to talk to someone in authority about the injustice. At last he finds a sympathetic listener in Mr. Sinclair of the Legal Aid Society. Sinclair renews Manuel's faith by explaining that people who believe in America can work together to make it the ideal land of the poem.

SUGGESTION

To make students more aware of the qualities that set Manuel apart, ask them to list adjectives that describe him—for example, *proud, resourceful,* and *persistent.* Then ask them to cite incidents from the story that demonstrate that he possesses each of the characteristics they have listed.

ANSWER KEY

1. G		9. D	
2. B		10. C	
3. A		11. F	
4. E		12. C	
5. D		13. E	
6. C		14. D	
7. A		15. E	
8. D			

Name: _____

Date: _____

The Land of Room Enough

To test your memory, match the descriptions in Column A with the characters in Column B. That will be easy if you became well acquainted with the people in the story.

Column A

1. _____ She was 45 and, so far, had had a life of hardships.

2. _____ He was a waiter who knew "all about everything."

3. _____ He was an idealistic boy, determined to make life better for his family.

4. _____ He was the family breadwinner, but was not very assertive.

5. _____ He was "young, scrubbed looking, and friendly."

6. _____ He had become cynical in America and wanted for himself the expensive articles he saw in the stores.

7. _____ He was the "real man of the family."

8. _____ Manuel thought this man would make a good mayor.

9. _____ He knew Manuel's poem and said people who believed in America could make it come true.

10. _____ He cheated his countrymen because he was greedy for money.

11. _____ He was Manuel's friend who liked to play the guitar and sing hillbilly songs.

12. _____ He pretended to be the landlord.

13. _____ He said any place was home as long as his family was there.

14. _____ He was from the Legal Aid Society and was willing to help Manuel.

15. _____ He had come to New York to help his sister-in-law in her photography shop.

Column B

A. Manuel

B. Mr. Dias

C. Mr. Jesepo

D. Mr. Sinclair

E. Papa Jorge

F. Enrique Dias

G. Mama

150 Great Short Stories

Pericles on 31st Street

Harry Mark Petrakis   *Moderate*

SYNOPSIS

The narrator, George, is a night bartender in Louis Debella's bar and prides himself on taking no part in customer disputes. Dan Ryan, a butcher; Olaf Johnson, a lunchroom owner; Sol Reidman, a tailor; and Bernard Klioris, a grocery-store owner, are regulars at the bar, having in common their landlord and a fondness for beer. A push-cart vendor, Nick Simonakis, also comes regularly but sits apart, sipping wine and criticizing the others. But when the landlord, Leonard Barsevick, makes an unwarranted increase of 15% in the men's store rent, Simonakis inspires them to stand up to their oppressor, calling on Pericles to give them strength!

SUGGESTION

Students should be made aware of the effectiveness of the title, combining an allusion to classical Greece with a reference to "here and now" on 31st Street. The title is humorous, too, since the affair in the bar is not of great historical importance, but a principle is at stake, all the same.

ANSWER KEY

1. Nick Simonakis
2. Olaf Johnson
3. Bernard Klioris
4. Sol Reidman
5. Dan Regan

6. Leonard Barsevick
7. Simonakis
8. Barsevick
9. Reidman
10. Johnson

Name: _____

Date: _____

Pericles on 31st Street

For questions 1–6, you are asked to match the character with the description. In questions 7–10, you are to state who is speaking.

THE CHARACTERS:

Dan Ryan	Bernard Klioris
Olaf Johnson	Nick Simonakis
Sol Reidman	Leonard Barsevick

1. _____ Is inclined to talk to himself, scorns beer drinkers, remembers ancient glories and long-dead heroes

2. _____ Has a huge belly, argues often with Sol, claims his lunch-room doesn't make much money

3. _____ Runs a grocery store, had a leaky roof, has a sad thin face, usually is confused when the others argue

4. _____ Is a tailor, thinks wine ruins a man's head, thinks they should have a delegation to speak to the landlord about the rent increase

5. _____ Owns a butcher shop, is a "heavy beer man," resents a remark about "inventing the wheelbarrow"

(continued)

Pericles on 31st Street (continued)

6. _____ Dresses fashionably, calls all his tenants his "friends," claims to be a man of his word, goes out with a girl who looks like Jayne Mansfield

7. _____ "A Greek would shoot him, but you are toads."

8. _____ "Believe me, boys, being a landlord and businessman is hell."

9. _____ "Judas, come to me only to sew your shroud."

10. _____ "Vulture, stop and eat on me, and I'll grind some glass for your salad."

Antaeus

Borden Deal   *Easy*

SYNOPSIS

The setting is a northern city during World War II, now crowded with new arrivals who have come for factory jobs. When T.J. and his family move into the narrator's building, he decides to introduce the newcomer to the other boys in his gang at their meeting place on the flat roof of a toy factory. A country boy, T.J. soon convinces the others that they can build a garden on the rooftop. By a laborious process, they do. But the owner discovers their grass plot and vows it will be shoveled off the next day. Determined that no one is "gonna lay a hand on his earth," T.J. begins to shovel it off himself, and the other boys help him finish the destruction.

SUGGESTION

Using a classical allusion, Deal says that T.J., like Antaeus in the myths, gained strength from his mother, Earth, and when he no longer had contact with the land, he "died." By recounting the story of Antaeus to the students, it's possible to show how effectively the allusion underlines the theme of the story. Students could also be made aware that the title of a story may offer clues to help them see the story's significance.

ANSWER KEY

1. slow, gentle voice; rural background; speech mannerisms; no name, just initials (any two)
2. land to grow crops
3. quiet confidence, assumption that he "belongs" and will be accepted
4. makes them more courageous, determined to prove their words
5. T.J. inspires them to keep going.
6. as a good leader, knew when to concede
7. more independent, his strong feeling that this is his land
8. He hasn't let any stranger touch his land.

Name: _____

Date: _____

Antaeus

If you can answer the following questions, you will have the answer to the question which heads this quiz.

1. _____ The narrator mentions several things that set T.J. apart from the other boys in the gang. Name two.

2. _____ What does T.J. miss in his new environment?

3. _____ What qualities of T.J.'s make the other boys like him almost in spite of themselves?

4. _____ When the other boys say that "they" wouldn't let them have a roof garden, T.J. replies, "I thought you said the roof was you-all's roof, that you-all could do anything you wanted to up here." What effect do his words have on the others?

5. Why don't the boys lose interest in the difficult project?

   _____

   _____

6. Why did T.J. agree to grow grass instead of vegetables?

   _____

   _____

7. Why is T.J. the only one to question the men's authority?

   _____

   _____

8. In a sense, T.J.'s final act of shoveling the earth off the roof is a victory for him. Why?

   _____

   _____

King David

Constance Fenimore Woolson   *Easy*

SYNOPSIS

Just after the Civil War, an idealistic young New Hampshire school-teacher, David King, goes to the South to teach the freed blacks. The settlement is Jubilee, where he, the only white man, lives in a cabin set apart from his neighbors, who have dubbed him "King David." At first he has so many pupils that he must divide them up—girls and women in the morning, men and boys in the afternoon, and old people at night—but he makes little progress despite his sincere efforts. Meanwhile, a neighboring plantation owner watches with amusement and scorn. Then a Northern "carpetbagger" undermines David completely, offering the black men whiskey and "pie in the sky." David goes back North, defeated.

SUGGESTION

Since "King David" was written shortly after the Civil War, it mirrors the contemporary attitudes and prejudices. To make students more aware of what they were, ask them to reread the passages that illustrate the following:

the attitude of David's New Hampshire neighbors toward the blacks;
the attitude of the retired planter, Ammerton;
David's own attitude toward his black neighbors;
the carpetbagger's attitude toward the blacks;
the blacks' attitude toward David and the Northern freedmen.

Then ask the students to share what they learned.

ANSWER KEY

1. C		9. A	
2. A		10. A	
3. D		11. C	
4. F		12. B	
5. A		13. A	
6. E		14. C	
7. C		15. B	
8. B			

Name: _____

Date: _____

King David

Column A contains descriptions of characters in the short story. Match them with the characters in Column B.

Column A

1. _____ Was an aristocratic retired planter

2. _____ Was an idealistic New England schoolmaster

3. _____ Gave the schoolmaster a parting gift of flowers

4. _____ Was the spokesman for the elderly blacks

5. _____ Asked to rent one of the planter's cotton fields and intended to pay blacks well to work it

6. _____ Had been a field hand; came to borrow the schoolmaster's axe

7. _____ Thought it was dangerous to educate the blacks

8. _____ Made much of his war record to impress the blacks; actually had never been in danger

9. _____ Went back to the North, defeated and discouraged

10. _____ Secretly found it difficult to associate with the blacks, but thought it was his duty to educate them

11. _____ Considered the schoolmaster a fanatic, but thought he was not like other Yankees

12. _____ Profited from his dealings with the blacks; encouraged them to drink

13. _____ Tried vainly to get advice from the retired planter

14. _____ Invited the teacher to join an association for their own "protection"

15. _____ Promised the blacks many things that he had no intention of delivering

Column B

A. David King

B. the "Captain"

C. Harnett Ammerton

D. Esther

E. Jim

F. Uncle Scipio

A Jury of Her Peers

Susan Glaspell

Moderate

SYNOPSIS

John Wright is dead—strangled—and his wife is being held in the county jail. Sheriff Peters, the County Attorney, the sheriff's wife, Hale (who discovered the body), and Hale's wife have come to the Wright farm. After talking to the women as if they were featherbrained, the men leave them alone in the kitchen and go about the house, looking for evidence. It is the women who actually find evidence that convinces them that Minnie Wright killed her husband because he had driven her beyond all endurance. By tacit consent, they conceal it—Minnie Wright has been tried and acquitted by a jury of her peers.

SUGGESTION

This is a good story to demonstrate how significant a title can be. In what sense are Mrs. Hale and Mrs. Peters Minnie Wright's peers? As a jury, what is their verdict?

ANSWER KEY

1. G	9. C
2. C	10. D
3. C	11. F
4. A	12. C
5. G	13. A
6. F	14. G
7. B	15. B
8. E	

A Jury of Her Peers

In Column A below are a number of descriptive phrases from the story; your task is to match them with the characters in Column B.

Column A

1. _____ The murdered man who died by strangulation

2. _____ The owner of the little canary which died from a broken neck

3. _____ Her kitchen was pretty untidy.

4. _____ The woman who had known the murdered man's wife since girlhood

5. _____ A strange silent man who didn't want a telephone because he thought people talked too much

6. _____ The County Attorney

7. _____ The sheriff's wife; she was small and thin

8. _____ The sheriff—big, genial, loud-voiced

9. _____ She sat in an old rocker, dazed, pleating her apron.

10. _____ He said, "Women are used to worrying over trifles."

11. _____ With an eye on his political future, he tried to flatter the women.

12. _____ She was once pretty and lively and sang in the choir.

13. _____ She pulled out the uneven stitches in the quilt and then resewed it.

14. _____ He didn't drink and kept his word and paid his debts, but he was a hard man.

15. _____ She knew what stillness was like because when she and her husband were homesteading in Dakota, her baby had died, and she had no other children.

Column B

A. Mrs. Hale

B. Mrs. Peters

C. Mrs. Wright

D. Mr. Hall

E. Mr. Peters

F. Mr. Henderson

G. John Wright

The Enemy

Pearl S. Buck   Moderate

SYNOPSIS

Sadao Hoki's father sent him to America to learn medicine and surgery. There he met another Japanese student, Hana, and married her when they had completed their studies and returned to Japan. Now, standing outside their beachfront house one foggy evening, they see a man crawl out of the sea toward them. He collapses. Hoki hurries to him and discovers he is a white man with a gunshot wound. Husband and wife agree it would be best to give him back to the sea—a prisoner of war, the enemy, an American. Instead, Hoki operates successfully; his wife bathes and feeds the man when the servants refuse, and, finally, Hoki helps him to escape, never sure all the while of his own motives.

SUGGESTION

The students need to be aware that Sadao and Hana Hoki are fighting prejudice in this story—that of their fellow Japanese, the servants, and even their own—in caring for the American. The question which should inspire a good class discussion is "why did they do it?"

ANSWER KEY

1. obviously considered it the place to get the best education

2. afraid they would be ruthless with no concern for the patient

3. criticized his food and house; thought his wife talked too much

4. repulsive

5. His father wouldn't have accepted anyone but a Japanese.

6. because he was white

7. The man has been in a prison camp. She doesn't want to believe he has been treated cruelly.

8. They are essential in an absolute state so that the ruler can deal with the opposition.

Reading Quiz:
Thinking It Over

Name: _____

Date: _____

The Enemy

Answer each question briefly.

1. Since Sadao's father wanted the best education for his son, what is significant about his sending him to America?

   _____

   _____

2. Why is the general reluctant to have his operation performed by a German-trained Japanese surgeon?

   _____

   _____

3. Sadao met his future wife at the home of his American professor who wanted to make certain the foreign students were not lonely. How did the students react?

   _____

   _____

4. What adjective does Hoki use in his own mind to describe white people?

   _____

   _____

5. Why did Sadao wait until he was sure Hana was Japanese before he allowed himself to fall in love with her?

   _____

   _____

6. Why wouldn't the servant wash the wounded man?

   _____

   _____

7. Why is Hana so troubled by red scars on the wounded man's neck?

   _____

   _____

8. What is Sadao's attitude toward the official assassins?

   _____

   _____

Price's Always Open

John O'Hara   *Moderate*

SYNOPSIS

Mr. Price, who had lost a leg in World War I, was a house painter in a summer resort, but used his veteran's bonus to open a lunchroom, popular in season with the young summer people whose families had been coming to the resort for years. On the fringe of "the crowd" is Jackie Gerard, invited to the Yacht Club dances because he plays the piano, but a "local" nonetheless. Louisa Leech, a haughty New Yorker, begins dating Sandy Hall after he knocks a fisherman "cold" in the lunchroom, but Jackie is interested in her and shows it. When Sandy knocks Jackie down, Price intervenes with a blackjack and kicks out the whole summer crowd.

SUGGESTION

O'Hara, particularly skillful in delineating the foibles of the upper middle class, shows here the attitude of a group of summer people toward the "townies"—an attitude sometimes snobbish and sometimes patronizing. Ask the students to describe their treatment of Jackie, Sandy's treatment of the Portuguese fisherman, and Sandy's description of the boxing match they attended.

ANSWER KEY

1. He is a "townie."

2. plays the piano

3. He refused a few times, and the others prefer it that way.

4. may not like the summer people or may feel Jackie really wouldn't be accepted

5. Jackie

6. thinks it is not quite good enough for her

7. scornfully kicks the man

8. a "nigger" and a "townie"

9. that he is yellow

10. Answers will vary.

Price's Always Open

Answer each of the following questions as briefly as possible.

1. Jackie Gerard attends the Yacht Club dances regularly, but one thing sets him apart from the other young people. What is it?

   _____

   _____

2. What special talent makes Jackie "socially acceptable"?

   _____

   _____

3. Why isn't Jackie invited to the smaller parties?

   _____

   _____

4. Why wouldn't Jackie's father approve of his going to the smaller parties?

   _____

   _____

5. When the young people bicker about the bill at Price's, who is most apt to pay for everyone?

   _____

   _____

(continued)

Price's Always Open (continued)

6. What is Louise Leech's attitude toward the resort?

_____

_____

7. What does Sandy Hall do after knocking down the fisherman that reveals his feelings about the man?

_____

_____

8. How does Sandy describe the two fighters in the boxing match?

_____

_____

9. What do Sandy and Louise say about one of the fighters, Bobbie Lawless, that Jackie resents?

_____

_____

10. In your opinion, why did Price throw the summer people out of his lunchroom?

_____

_____

Bibliography

1. *Adventures in Appreciation*—Loban and Olmstead, eds. (New York: Harcourt, Brace, and World, Inc., 1952)

2. *Adventures in English Literature*—Inglis, Stauffer, and Larsen, eds. (New York: Harcourt, Brace, and World, Inc., 1952)

3. *After Appomattox: The Image of the South in Its Literature (1865-1900)* Gene Baro, ed. (New York: Corinth Books, 1963)

4. *America in Literature—The Midwest*—Ronald Szymanski, ed. (New York: Charles Scribner's Sons, 1979)

5. *America in Literature—The West*—Peter Monahan, ed. (New York: Charles Scribner's Sons, 1979)

6. *American Local-Color Stories*—Warful and Orians, eds. (New York: American Book Co., 1941)

7. *America's Literature*—Hart and Gohdes, eds. (New York: Holt, Rinehart, and Winston, 1955)

8. *An Anthology of Famous American Stories*—Burrell and Cerf, eds. (New York: The Modern Library, 1955)

9. *Angels and Awakenings*—M. Cameron Grey, ed. (New York: Doubleday, 1980)

10. *At Your Own Risk*—Charlotte K. Brooks, ed. (New York: Holt, Rinehart, and Winston, 1968)

11. *Best American Short Stories, 1970*—Foley and Burnett, eds. (Boston: Houghton Mifflin, 1970)

12. *Best Short Stories by Negro Writers*—Langston Hughes, ed. (Boston: Little, Brown and Co., 1970)

13. *Beyond the Pale and Other Stories* by William Trevor (New York: The Viking Press, 1981)

14. *Cities*—Charlotte K. Brooks, ed. (New York: Holt, Rinehart, and Winston, 1968)

15. *Classic Irish Short Stories*—Frank O'Connor, ed. (Oxford: Oxford University Press, 1986)

16. *Collected Stories: Frank O'Connor* (New York: Alfred A. Knopf, 1981)

17. *Collected Stories of Jean Stafford* (New York: Farrar, Straus, and Giroux, 1969)

18. *Endless Horizons*—Bailey and Leavett, eds. (New York: American Book Co., 1956)

19. *Fables for Our Time and Famous Poems Illustrated*—James Thurber (New York: Harper & Row, 1940)

20. *Fifty Best American Short Stories, (1915-1939)*—E.J.H. O'Brien, ed. (Boston: Houghton Mifflin, 1938)

21. *Fifty Modern Stories*—Thomas M.H. Blair, ed. (Evanston, IL: Row, Peterson and Company, 1960)

22. *Fifty Years of the American Short Story - 2 vols.*—William Abrahams, ed. (Garden City, N.Y.: Doubleday & Co., 1960)

23. *Great Canadian Short Stories*—Alec Lucas, ed. (New York: Dell Publishing Co., 1971)

24. *Here and Now*—Fred Morgan, ed. (New York: Harcourt, Brace, and World, 1968)

25. *I've Got a Name*—Charlotte K. Brooks, ed. (New York: Holt, Rinehart and Winston, 1968)

26. *Man and His Measure*—Francis Connolly, ed. (New York: Harcourt, Brace, and World, 1964)

27. *Medicine for Melancholy*—by Ray Bradbury (Garden City, N.Y.: Doubleday & Co., 1959)

28. *Moonlight Traveler*—Philip Van Doren Stern, ed. (Garden City, N.Y.: Doubleday, Doran and Co., Inc., 1943)

29. *Morley Callaghan's Stories*—(Toronto: MacMillan, 1959)

30. *The Old West in Fiction*—Irwin R. Blacker, ed. (New York: Ivan Oblensky, Inc., 1961)

31. *Our English Heritage*—Bailey and Leavell, eds. (New York: The American Book Co., 1952)

32. *The Outnumbered*—Charlotte Brooks, ed. (New York: Delacorte Press, 1967)

33. *The Oxford Book of Short Stories*—V.S. Pritchett, ed. (New York: Oxford University Press, 1981)

34. *Reading for Pleasure*—Bennett Cerf, ed. (New York: Harper & Brothers, 1957)

35. *Representative Modern Short Stories*—Alexander Jessup, ed. (New York: The MacMillan Co., 1929)

36. *Saturday Evening Post Stories*, 1959 (Boston: Little, Brown and Co., 1959)

37. *Selected Tales and Poems of Edgar Allen Poe* (New York: Walter J. Black, Inc., 1943)

38. *The Short Stories of de Maupassant*—Guy de Maupassant (New York: The Book League of America, 1941)

39. *Complete Stories of Flannery O'Connor* (New York: Farrar, Straus and Giroux, 1971)

40. *The Short Stories of Ernest Hemingway* (New York: Charles Scribner's Sons, 1938)

41. *Story Jubilee*—Whit and Hallie Burnett, eds. (Garden City, N.Y.: Doubleday & Co., 1965)

42. *Ten Contemporary Polish Stories*—Edmond Ordon, ed. (Detroit: Wayne University Press, 1958)

43. *A Treasury of Short Stories*—Bernardine Kielty, ed. (Kingsport, TN: Kingsport Press, Inc., 1947)

44. *Twenty-Three Modern Stories*—Barbara Howes, ed. (New York: Random House, 1963)

45. *Values in Literature*—Chase, Jewett, and Evans, eds. (New York: Houghton Mifflin, 1965)

46. *Winesburg, Ohio*—by Sherwood Anderson (New York: The Modern Library, 1947)

47. *The Works of Robert Louis Stevenson*—(New York: Walter J. Black, Inc., 1926)

48. *World of the Short Story*—(Boston: Houghton Mifflin Co., 1986)

Index of Authors

Index of Stories